Working with Parents:
A Whole-school Approach

16/3/94

Working with Parents:
A Whole-school Approach

John Bastiani

NFER-NELSON

Published by The NFER-NELSON Publishing Company Ltd.,
Darville House, 2 Oxford Road East,
Windsor, Berkshire SL4 1DF, England.

First published 1989
© 1989, John Bastiani

British Library Cataloguing in Publication Data
Parents and teachers.
  3, Working with Parents: a whole-school approach
  1. Great Britain. Schools. Relations with parents
  I. Bastiani, John, 1941–
  371.1'03'0941

Phototypeset by David John Services Ltd, Slough
Printed by Dotesios Printers Ltd, Trowbridge, Wiltshire

ISBN 0 7005 1183 0
Code 8317 02 4

Contents

Acknowledgements

The completion of the series 'Parents and Teachers' brings to an end a busy period of writing in which I have tried to sort out and learn lessons from more than a decade of development work with teachers and parents. As a result, I am now in a good position to see clearly how much I owe to others. I should, therefore, like to thank the following people.

All the teachers I have worked with, from different parts of Britain, from whom I have learned a great deal, for sharing their time and experience with me so generously. In spite of all that has happened to them in recent years, the vast majority of teachers have maintained a level of integrity and commitment to their work that is nothing less than remarkable.

All the parents that I have listened to and who have worked with me on various projects. In spite of all that is said to the contrary in the popular press, the vast majority of parents take their job very seriously and try hard to do their best for their children. As a parent myself, I know that this is easier said than done, especially at present.

On a more particular note, I should like to thank two colleagues, Janet Atkin and Jackie Goode, with whom I have worked so productively and in such a human way on so many occasions. I should also like to thank the group of teachers who formed the basis of the Community Education Working Party, from whom I learned a great deal about collaborative working and the development of thoughtful practice. They, and others familiar with our earlier work at Nottingham, will see echoes of our long association at several places in this book.

Peter Adams, for illustrations provided by his top juniors at Maple Cross Primary School, Herts.

Peter Hannon and Angela Jackson, for material from the Belfield Reading Project.

The Welsh Consumer Council, for an illustration from their bilingual guide to schools for parents.

Finally, I should like, yet again, to acknowledge the skill and helpfulness of my secretary, Jill Cleaver, who could be forgiven for thinking that I write at least two books each week! This time she has had to cope not only with the usual indecipherable scripts that I hand over to her, but with my well-meaning attempts to get away from the normal conventions of style and layout, to produce a book that is both highly readable and easy to use.

Introduction

This book completes a series of three accounts linked by the generic title of *Parents and Teachers*. For, although each of the volumes is very different in form and content, they are linked by a common, underlying philosophy. Central to this is the view that there can only be a fundamental improvement in home–school relations when schools are able to identify parental needs, wishes and experience and are willing to respond to them in a spirit of practical partnership.

The series as a whole tries to make a substantial and useful contribution to the work of schools in this area. The first book *Perspectives on Home–School Relations*, brings together a collection of material, much of which has been specially written. It offers a challenging view of the field from an angle that recognizes the expectations and experience of parents. It's main purpose is to provoke a better understanding of complex home–school issues in ways that enable a critical review of existing practice to be carried out and which also suggest a number of constructive lines of development.

The second book, *From Policy to Practice*, carries on where the first leaves off. For as well as exploring some of the major concerns of both policymakers and practitioners, it gives considerable emphasis to the problems of trying to translate good ideas into effective action, a task which is developed in a more practical way in the present account.

Although sharing the same underlying philosophy about family–school relations, *Working with Parents: A Whole-school Approach* adopts a *totally* different style and approach, to enable it to make an independent contribution to the development of home– school thinking and practice. It has also been written in a way that enables it to tackle the concerns and engage the experience of hard-pressed teachers, who currently have a great deal on their plates. For this reason, I have tried to write a book that is both accessible and useful, that recognizes the pressures which schools and teachers are under, but which does not duck the important issues that the improvement of home–school relations inevitably raises. Above all, I have tried to communicate a spirit of down to earth practical idealism, relevant to teachers working in a wide range of institutions, which is tolerant of different attitudes and approaches. This seems preferable to either a narrow evangelism or the assumption that there are always solutions to all of our problems.

Another distinctive feature of this account is its insistence that home–school relations should be viewed, not just in terms of the dealings between individual teachers and parents, but as a major task to be tackled by the school *as a whole*, through the development of appropriate policies and practices, drawn from a range of competing views about what should be done and how teachers should go about it. Within such a 'whole school approach', the development of more positive attitudes and relationships is only a part, however important, of the wider professional task of developing relevant organizational forms and effective ways of working.

The organization of the book tries to bring its two major themes together in a down to earth way. The opening section sets home–school relations firmly in the context of contemporary issues and events, identifies some of the main concerns of the book and illustrates its general approach.

Part Two explores and illustrates relationships between families and schools as an important arena for organizational growth and professional development. Through its emphasis upon individual schools and the families of the children they teach, it illustrates different ways in which parents can become more involved in the life and work of the school. This emphasis is seen as a key element in a school's efforts to develop and change in this area.

Working with Parents gives considerable emphasis, as the title suggests, to the identification of a wide variety of practical forms of home–school activity. Its focus shifts from a wide-angled view of the possible arrangements of the programme as a whole, with the characteristic challenges and problems of planning, organization and evaluation, to a close-up examination of a number of particular activities. It also ranges from a consideration of some of the most obvious wide-spread and basic practices to a brief look at a number of interesting current developments.

Part Four concentrates attention on a number of embryonic, problematic and unresolved issues in the field, that acknowledge family perspectives and experience, where both professional thinking is under-developed and practical initiatives needed.

Underneath this obvious and deliberate structure, considerable reinforcement is given to particular ideas and values by the unplanned use of frequently repeated words and phrases, a process that I have only become fully aware of with the book's completion. So, for example, I find I have mentioned on a number of occasions the need to 'strike a balance' between competing attitudes and approaches, between the different needs of families and schools and the wide ranging nature of home–school philosophies, policies and practice.

Similarly, I find I have drawn attention several times to the relationship between home–school rhetoric and its practice. For our fine words are not always matched by effective action; we do not always practise what we preach, or recognize the possible discrepancies between the two, which is necessary if they are to be brought closer together.

Finally, I have made great use of the idea of 'appropriateness' at many places in this account, reinforcing the view that it is crucial for all schools to tailor work to their own particular needs, circumstances and experience, rather than dealing in bland, general formulae and attempted solutions. This is something, however, that schools can never achieve on their own, but only through the growing understanding, the sympathetic cooperation and the involvement of the parents and families of the children they teach.

1 Getting Things into Focus

The current scene

Relations between families and schools, between teachers, parents and pupils have, in a fairly short period of time, become an important contemporary concern. To a large extent, this is because such issues figure prominently on the agendas of politicians, professionals and parents alike.

For *politicians*, such an interest can be seen against a background of reducing public expenditure and influence, in getting better value for money and in making public institutions more accountable to consumer pressure. Above all, it has meant bringing public services within the aegis of the government's political and economic strategies, through the increasingly centralist direction and control of policies and resources.

From a political viewpoint, parents have become an important lobby, a key sounding board for educational policy and a source of electoral support. Characteristically, recent governments and politicians of all parties, have tended to see home–school matters in terms of general policies and enabling legislation rather than, say, the skilful use of resources or the quality of relationships between teachers and parents. So the 1980, 1981, 1986 and 1988 Education Acts have attempted to chart some of the parental rights of consumers, have given them certain kinds of limited choices as individuals and, more recently, some collective powers to opt out of local authority control. Parents have also been consistently given a larger formal stake in the management of schools themselves.

For *professionals* in the education service, parents can be seen to have moved, as a result of their own and the government's efforts, from a shadowy position on the margins of the educational process, to a position nearer the centre of the stage. Although not necessarily greeted with wild enthusiasm by all teachers, the crucial influence of parents upon their children's educational achievements has been widely recognized. This has been supported by a steady accumulation of research evidence which has put this beyond reasonable doubt and has served to confirm what many teachers know in their bones as the result of their daily experience in classrooms.

Increasingly, too, teacher–parent relationships have been the object of serious consideration by teacher associations, a few LEAs, several significant home– school projects and, above all, individual schools. As a result, a number of policy and discussion documents have emerged, in which uplifting rhetoric about 'partnership' is tempered by strong reservations about increasing demands upon teachers beyond reasonable limits, together with a new realism about the extent to which professionally-led change is possible in the current climate.

A few years ago the dispute between the government and most of the teaching profession had also brought to a head a number of difficult and unresolved issues concerning the nature of teachers' duties and performance. Although a temporary truce appears, at least on the surface, to have been achieved, it is difficult to say what the longer term effects will be in terms of changed commitment and professional attitudes. Certainly many teachers and families have found themselves experiencing rapidly changing and contradictory interests and loyalties, which now appear to be harnessed to a combined lack of enthusiasm for the government's proposals, particularly for opting out of local authority control and for testing at all ages.

For *parents*, the last decade has seen slow, but unspectacular progress in combatting the notion that their children's education was 'not really any of their business' or that their contact with their children's schools should be very limited, except as fund-raisers or extra pairs of hands in an emergency. By getting organized, in national and local groups, parents have been able to exert a steady pressure upon schools and the system, to oblige them to recognize parental rights and expectations and to become more responsive to parental needs and interests.

More recently, the focus of parental anxiety and concern has shifted from the alleged inadequacies of the teaching profession, the incomprehensibility of modern teaching methods or the breakdown of teacher authority (often the result of media hype) to a growing concern about the quality of provision in their children's schools, at the level of staffing, buildings and equipment. Indeed, this increasingly critical stance, which parent organizations have adopted in the face of current proposals and consistent under resourcing, has caused the government to rapidly distance itself from those parental representative bodies which it had previously assumed would provide unswerving loyalty and uncritical support!

So home–school relations are now firmly on the agenda of politicians, professionals and parents, albeit in different and changing ways. This is true literally as a consequence of cumulative legislation and formal opportunities for parents to be involved in the life and work of schools. It is also true metaphorically. Parents have become a strongly-felt, though often unseen, presence in the plans of politicians, in the daily work of education offices and in the work of schools. Above all, it has become necessary to accept that the creation and support of effective family–school relationships is a necessary and legitimate concern, *not* an optional extra, as it was previously considered to be.

The importance of parents

Such an important shift of attitude, with all its implications, seems to draw upon three main sets of beliefs and values:

Parents have important *rights* (and corresponding obligations) increasingly encased in law, concerning the education and development of their children and the way it is provided for. This seems to be the major focus in the present government's view.

There is increasing recognition of the tangible benefits that result from actively enlisting the *support and involvement* of parents in their children's schooling. Indeed, in the present climate many schools[1] could not survive without the kinds of help that they have come to depend upon. Whilst this most obviously applies to financial and other forms of material support, there is now also widespread professional acceptance of the value of parental involvement in aspects of the educational process itself, as the beneficial effects of parental support for children's reading has demonstrated so clearly over the last decade or so.

Less obviously, there is a steadily growing acknowledgement of the value of parents as an important educational *resource*. There are many things that parents know and can do, that are of immense value in the education of their children, which schools are only just beginning to recognize, let alone utilize.

Whilst this area is the least developed of the three, and rather overshadowed by contemporary events of a very different kind, there is still a growing body of commitment and experience in this area, particularly in the pre-school and special needs areas, in which parents are acknowledge in their important role as *educators* themselves.

'There's more to it than meets the eye!'

Until a few years ago, the study and practice of home–school relationships was not really given much serious attention. It might be seen as a rather distant concern of planners and government researchers; it was established as a minor topic about which teachers in training wrote flabby essays; for schools and practising teachers, however, it was regarded as an optional extra, to be taken-up or ignored, according to personal philosophy or experience. One of the end results of this is that you will probably have received little or no training for your work with parents, either before you entered the profession, or since. Developing the ability to 'handle parents' is something that, until recently, has been assumed to be learned naturally, on the job, over a period of time and, apart from one or two mildly traumatic experiences with individual parents, without too much difficulty.

---

1   'School' is here, as elsewhere in this account, taken as a form of shorthand for a whole range of educational institutions, centres and units, catering for learners of all ages, conditions and backgrounds, predominantly, but certainly not exclusively, relating to the age of compulsory schooling.

Recently, however, such a view has come to be seen as both inaccurate and unhelpful. For relations between families and schools, teachers and parents are currently known, in the jargon, as being 'problematic'. For instance, despite the cosy and uplifting rhetoric about partnership and cooperation and the steady spread of 'good practice', home–school relationships in the real world are inevitably characterized by elements of underlying tension and by intractable dilemmas. Schools *are* competitive places and the scramble for achievement and success divides parents just as surely as it divides pupils. So, too, families and schools are very different kinds of institution. Although there is common ground each has its own, sometimes contradictory, concerns and responsibilities. If you have children of your own in school, you will know just what I mean!

Parents and families are an important influence upon school and classroom life, even where their actual presence is somewhat silent and invisible. They occupy a powerful place in teacher lore and staffroom mythology, which often contrasts strongly with what those same parents are *really* like. Such stereotypes can often have a crucial impact upon the way teachers think and act about home–school matters. In the 'real world', for example, parents as a group are seldom as united, as interfering or as unappreciative of a school's genuine efforts, as they are in the demonology.

So, too, in their dealings with their children's schools, many parents encounter a system that 'speaks with forked tongue!'. For home–school relations, like much educational life, is an area where our fine words and our actions do not always match- up. Good intentions are not a guarantee of effective practice. This account tries to recognize these differences in an honest way, preferring genuine improvements, however unspectacular or limited, to empty rhetoric.

Educational and social change

Home–school relations take place against a broader backcloth of social and educational change. This short introduction has already referred to the present government's desire to harness schooling to its own view of social improvement in general and to a more efficient economy in particular, and of its willingness to directly intervene in the work of schools and teachers to bring this about. An effective philosophy of home–school relations, in addition to recognizing the changing circumstances of schools and teachers, will similarly need to recognize the changing realities of family and community life.

Any case for improving home–school relationships starts with the view that the effective education of the next generation requires us to recognize the needs, wishes and experience of children and their families. Put another way, it is both an educational and a professional nonsense for schools (or individuals within them) to operate in ignorance of, and isolation from, the families they serve and the neighbourhoods in which they have been located. In practice, this is complicated by important and widespread changes in the structure and organization of both family and community life. Arrangements for bringing up children are now very diverse, as class teachers and form tutors are constantly finding out, with widely-differing values and styles of parenting associated with such a task.

These are also reflected in the changing face and lifestyles of neighbourhoods, particularly in our large cities.

Taken together, these changes represent a shifting pattern in the relationships between the major institutions of family, school and work, whose effects are felt, often painfully, by institutions and individuals alike. Such a shift also represents a series of both challenges and opportunities, many of which are taken up later. From whichever angle you look at it, one thing is clear – there has never been a greater need for schools and families to cooperate and, where possible, to support one another, in the interests of the children for whom they are both responsible, albeit in different ways.

The 'Nottingham style'

During the last 15 years I have been working with teachers in very different ways in a wide range of settings. As a result of this experience, something has emerged which is akin to a 'Nottingham style', which contains elements both of a philosophy and a way of working. It's basic ingredients include the following.

The need to develop thinking and practice *together*. Any attempt to separate the two is artificial and, in the end, counter productive. In particular, reflecting on your own experience, (and that of immediate colleagues) is especially productive.

Improving home–school relations is a job for *all* schools and teachers, not an optional extra for those who have the inclination. In reality, all schools contain widely- differing attitudes and experience with regard to home–school matters, which must be acknowledged if we are to get anywhere. For this reason, and others, 'preaching to the converted' is a rather unproductive business.

Relationships between families and schools necessarily involve tension and conflict, as well as opportunities for partnership and mutual support. This applies just as much to 'better' relationships as to existing ones, although the actual problems may differ. A healthy scepticism about these things is always handy!

Teachers have much to offer, and to learn from each other. This also applies across the great sectarian divides of the nursery/infant, primary/secondary and special education sectors. Whilst there *are* special features and important differences that must be recognized, the common ground is more extensive and fertile.

In the past, too, teacher education has probably given too much attention to the introduction of new, different ideas and practices and not enough to the development of existing ones, but both are important.

Above all, our trademark has been the importance we always attach to the need to consider, and respond to, the perspectives and experience of *parents* themselves. There can be no real progress in the field of home–school relations if it is regarded as a solely professional concern.

The development of home–school relations: whose job?

This book is based upon the view, backed up by considerable experience, that ultimately it is individual schools and teachers who must be the most important focus in any attempt to improve home–school relations. It is, however, far too big and complex a task for schools to tackle alone. In the end, success in this area needs the combined efforts of the education service as a whole, with its wider perspectives and its command of additional human and material resources, its potential for providing knowledge and practical support, drawn from the advisory and support services.

It also goes without saying that, although the developments that are envisaged might be professionally-led there can be no real change without the genuine involvement of parents and families themselves. The improvement of home–school relations calls, by definition, for the education service to become more responsive to the needs, wishes and experience of parents and children and for the development of an honest partnership that recognizes important differences as well as shared concerns.

Role for government, DES and other national bodies

- Introducing legislation for the management of family–school relations
- The establishment of a broad national policy and priorities – with regional variations where appropriate
- The development of general guidelines and useful resources on a national basis
- The identification of training needs and the adoption of appropriate kinds of support – especially for the initial training of teachers
- Taking major research and development initiatives. This includes the monitoring of existing policy and practice (including data gathered by HMI in school inspections as well as the support of growth in areas of emerging concern.

Role for LEAs

- Tailoring national policies, and developing their own, to take account of: local needs and circumstances, e.g. the needs of urban/rural, multicultural/bilingual communities; the needs of specific groups, e.g. ethnic minorities, the parents of special needs children etc.
- Workable focus for a general review of policy and practice followed by the dissemination of good ideas and effective practice
- Appropriate level at which schools can make good use of: the advisory and support services; their human and material resources, e.g. in running a school-based INSET day, printing materials for parents etc.
- The necessary focus for certain policies, both general and selectively applied, e.g. home–school liaison schemes, posts of responsibility for

home–school matters, the release of teachers to pursue home–school tasks etc.

- The creation of a mediation service for the use of both parents and schools. It would provide information and advice, together with conciliation facilities to tackle disputes between families and schools.

Role for individual schools

- There is extensive agreement, reinforced by cumulative experience, that the individual institution (school, nursery unit, centre, etc.) is the most effective focus for genuine change. For it is here where: teachers, pupils and parents meet, and interact; the connections between good relationships and organizational needs are most acutely felt; the need for effective practical arrangements is sharpest.
- There is plenty of evidence, of different kinds, that effective home–school relationships require recognition of the peculiarly local, neighbourhood flavour to its: characteristic issues and pressing concerns; key communications strategies and styles; key locations, personalities, sub-cultural values etc.
- By definition, 'grass-roots' development can only take place here. It is only at this level that: the complex needs and wishes of parents can be acknowledged and met; specific needs can be identified and, above all, policies and practices influenced 'from the bottom-up', both by individuals and small groups.
- An ideal focus is provided for certain kinds of small-scale pioneering and development work. This is particularly valuable for voluntary initiatives and for creative opportunism, although it also applies to a wide range of essentially practical developments.

Improving home-school relations: the ten commandments!

The development of more effective home-school policies and practice needs to combine, in a unique way, the characteristic features and special problems of home-school relations, as they concern teachers, parents and pupils respectively; and the lessons that can be learned from our growing experience of trying to change educational institutions and processes elsewhere, in the fields of curriculum and organizational reform, and in professional development.

An attempt has been made to combine these sources of understanding and experience, in the following, highly condensed form:

- Improving home-school relationships brings important mutual benefits to children and their families, to schools and their communities.
- To make this possible, it is necessary to understand parents' perspectives and their experience - to be able to see the world from *their* point of view.
- There is much that parents know and can do, that could be of great value in their children's education. This knowledge and skill remains largely unrecognized and almost entirely untapped.
- Parents' attitudes towards education, and their experience of their children's schools, vary in interesting and important ways.
- Relationships between families and schools are not as straightforward as they are often made out to be. Families and schools *are* different kinds of institutions. Important differences and inevitable tensions must be recognized and tackled - *not* swept under the carpet.
- Better home-school relations necessarily involve children, as well as teachers and parents.
- There is, regrettably, no simple formula for, or short-cuts to, improving home-school relations. As elsewhere, change requires some risk and much effort.
- For the real growth of home-school relations, thinking and practice must develop together.
- Most teachers realize that there are significant gains to be made by improving home-school practice. This involves much more, however, than the development of positive attitudes. It calls for the development of new skills and new practices as well.
- If families and schools are to work together in an active partnership, school and teachers will have to change, as well as families and parents.

2 Developing a Whole–school Approach

Although it is frequently referred to with obvious approval, the notion of a 'whole-school' approach remains a rather vague, undefined set of ideas. So this section begins with a brief attempt to identify a few of its essential values and characteristics, as a background to a more detailed look at a number of possible management and development strategies.

Elements of a whole-school approach

Such an approach implies a broad, coherent philosophy, thoughtful leadership and professional activity, a concern for the quality of its achievements and the widespread involvement and general job satisfaction of those who work in it, or are associated with it. More specifically, a whole school approach incorporates: (1) A broad vision, worked out through discussion, of the way things might be, linked to a clear picture of the way things are, which is rooted in evidence and shared experience. (2) The importance of recognizing important differences of personality, attitude and experience. There is a place here both for the seeking of a broad consensus, where this seems appropriate, and for the constructive exploitation of useful differences of philosophy, policy and practice, where this is more productive. (3) A key point of reference is to the needs and interests of the school and its members as a whole, rather than to narrow or sectional interests. This implies a corresponding *commitment* to the whole enterprise, rather than to a particular part of it. (4) A broad and varied range of opportunities for participation and involvement, which are not tied to a rigid status hierarchy or to an orthodox viewpoint, but to the completion of agreed tasks and the implementation of new ideas and practices.

Although effective schooling is here recognized as a team effort, it does require the allocation of tasks and responsibilities to be made on a clear, fair basis. For example, an understanding should be developed of the links between the implementation of more effective arrangements for teaching and learning (curriculum), the development of the school as a thinking and caring community (organization) and the growth of the kinds of personal and professional relationships that make this possible. Above all, a whole school approach can only work if it manages to achieve a successful blend of educational idealism with a strong sense of practical realism.

It is sometimes suggested that a whole-school approach is only possible with directive leadership, wide consensus or in smaller, mainly primary, schools. This, as can be seen, is not my view, neither has it been my experience. What is important, however, here as elsewhere, is that different types of schools, in different settings, will need to develop their own structures and ways of working that grow out of a consideration of their own circumstances and experience.

The organization and management of home–school relations

Key tasks and issues

The whole of section two draws upon a number of issues that are part of our cumulative experience of education generally (such as curriculum development and organizational reform). It applies them specifically to the organization and management of home–school relations, which has its own characteristics, opportunities and problems. Nowhere is this clearer than in the identification of key management tasks, within a whole school approach.

The management of home–school relations will need to:
- establish clear goals, policies and priorities;
- find ways of handling the different views and experience of parents, pupils and teachers, (and the inevitable tensions between them);
- identify and respond to special needs in this area;
- monitor and evaluate the existing programme; and
- facilitate and support appropriate innovation and development, in line with the school's changing aims and the changing expectations of parents. These tasks are taken up and explored at various places throughout this account.

There are a number of overlapping issues that, sooner or later, will need to be considered as part of a whole school approach to the improvement of home–school relations. At some times these are experienced as sharply-felt contradictions, or dilemmas to be tackled; at others, they appear as straightforward choices, or priorities. Here, however, they are represented as wide-ranging strategic themes and issues requiring broad consideration, but which need to be resolved in a practical way (Table 2.1). They are also a way of drawing attention to problems of balance and emphasis. This will, inevitably, be placed differently by school staffs and individual teachers, according to philosophy, circumstances and past experience.

Key roles and responsibilities

The organization and management of a home–school programme often suffers from a number of common weaknesses, whose effects are heightened because they are often found together. In the first place, home–school matters tend not to occupy a place on the agenda of teachers in ways that are likely to lead to a review of present efforts, of short- or longer-term planning or, above all, a broad

Table 2.1

Consensus	v	*Pluralism*
Basic, shared assumptions and values/common ground		Widely-differing beliefs about key issues/diverse approaches
How far is an agreed basic philosophy an essential *requirement* of an effective home–school programme?		Should important differences be defended? Can they sometimes be *utilized* constructively?
School policy	v	*Voluntary activity*
Important when:		Important when:
Cornerstone of school's philosophy and approach		Marker of acceptable areas of difference and diversity
Based on generally agreed and widely-accepted practice		As a strategy for small-scale pioneering work
Involving, or applying to, *all* staff		Signals a low priority area
Essential to effectiveness of programme		
Basic programme	v	*Areas of growth and development*
Different functions:		Different functions:
Laying the foundations		Developing existing attitudes and practices
School-wide activities		Specific innovations and projects
Routine monitoring and maintenance		Pioneering work
Periodic review		Short- or longer-term development
Initiative	v	*Response*
Taking the lead		Responding to the needs, interests and experience of parents and families
Professional tasks and responsibilities		Encouraging grass roots development
Planning-led activity		Picking-up spontaneous opportunities
The needs of parents – as a whole	v	*Special needs*
The needs of parents – as opposed to those of schools		Identifying and catering for special needs, groups and circumstances
Responding to basic, common needs and circumstances		Working with minority groups and interests

and systematic analysis of a school's efforts *as a whole*. Indeed home–school relations are often experienced as a series of unrelated practices and events, or as mini-crises as the school calendar moves relentlessly forward through a predictable pattern and rhythm.

Secondly, the actual distribution of teacher responsibility in home–school matters is usually entangled in the status hierarchy. Schools are often nervous in their dealings with the 'outside world' and this is mirrored in the arrangements that are made for communication and contact between teachers and parents. For 'dealing with parents' often appears to be regarded as a responsibility that ordinary tutors and class teachers cannot be entrusted with. In many schools, therefore, it remains tightly under the wing of house or year heads in secondary schools and headteachers and their deputies in primary schools.

Finally, only a relatively small number of LEAs and individual schools have created special roles or posts of responsibility, whose main purpose is to extend or improve the effectiveness of home–school arrangements. There are, as most readers will know, some very significant exceptions to this general pattern, mainly in the primary sector, where such posts are part of a positive discrimination strategy in social priority areas.

Such criticisms also imply a number of corrective strategies and constructive alternatives, which will be identified and illustrated later in this section and throughout this account. For the moment, however, it might help to identify a range of activities and responsibilities which need to be effectively managed in any home–school programme.

Some basic tasks and responsibilities[2]

- Establishing relationships with new and prospective parents.
- Ensuring continuity through transition from: nursery to infant; infant/junior; primary/secondary; and lower/middle/upper school.
- Communicating with parents about the life and work of the school generally and in relation to special developments, e.g. new forms of pupil grouping, GCSE.
- Organizing activities in the home–school programme, e.g. regular features – parents' evenings, fund raising and social events; or, special events, e.g. exhibitions and educational workshops, projects and activities.
- Dovetailing home–school activities into the school's careers education and guidance programme, where appropriate.
- Dealing with acute personal and social problems specific to individual pupils and families.

---

2   This section corresponds, in many ways, to the 'Key Moments . . .' theme in Section 4. Here home–school events are viewed from a mainly organizational perspective and interests. In Section 4 the emphasis is upon the perspectives of pupils and families. A comparison between the two can often produce useful insights into the tensions between families and schools.

- Initiating training and professional development in relation to pastoral work in general and home–school matters in particular.
- Acting as a focus for contact with other agencies concerned with the education, health and welfare of children and young people.
- Linking, up, via families, of the school with its wider community.

How are these activities organized in *your* school? Who is responsible and on what basis? Do you think these responsibilities could be distributed more effectively or on a different basis?

Home–school liaison: whose job?

In considering this question, tasks and responsibilities have been grouped under the following three headings. Senior Management – within a recognizable system of accountability and school improvement. Class teachers or form tutors – to focus attention on the basic foundations of the system and the basic features of the home–school programme. Posts of special responsibility – as a means of identifying what could be done with a sharpening of effort and a concentration of resources. This framework is offered (here, as elsewhere) not as a blueprint but as a starting point for discussion and further consideration.

Senior management

The model of management adopted here is that such staff should function as senior members of a team. Their true job is to facilitate and support, rather than coerce and direct.

In the home–school field, however, there are many areas where senior staff are not the 'experts'. Other members of staff, for example, may live in the neighbourhood, or be otherwise involved in the life of the community through youth work, local clubs and societies etc. Such colleagues have valuable knowledge and experience which can be an important asset to the school. But it can also challenge the traditional pattern of authority or deeply entrenched staffroom mythologies.

So it is the function of senior management to bring about, from their own efforts and from supporting others, a clear system of accountability – clear, that is, to parents as well as teachers. It should be responsive to the needs of 'external audiences' and rooted in evidence of its effectiveness. They should also bring about the kind of leadership that embodies a wider view, not only of how things are but of how they might be; a management style that enables a school to translate its developing philosophy into appropriate policies and effective practice; the coordination of effort and experience; and the facilitation of, and support for, development and change.

Form tutors: class teachers

Unless they have been reduced to mere functionaries who mark registers, form tutors (and, even more so, class teachers in primary schools) are likely to have unrivalled personal knowledge of individual pupils. Because of this it makes important sense, especially to parents, to make form tutors and class teachers the bedrock and foundation of a devolved system of responsibility for home–school matters. In schools which are relatively informal and open, or who try to mitigate the worst excesses of rigid hierarchies, this already happens. In others, this might require a shift of policy and direction, together with the adoption of appropriate measures to strengthen the role of form tutor or class teacher.

Such a role would incorporate all the following. The obvious locus for a school's primary responsibility for home– school communication, the first and most personal link in a two-way pattern of contact. A responsibility, with the support of both parents and colleagues, for tackling problems and anxieties concerning individual pupils as they arise, together with the task of initiating special arrangements and monitoring their effectiveness. The need, for most schools, to strengthen the role of tutors and class teachers by devolving responsibility, e.g. for writing letters to parents, arranging home visits, participating in case conferences etc., and, providing appropriate encouragement and practical support, e.g. alleviation of other duties, peer support, INSET experience etc.

Posts of special responsibility

A wide range of home–school liaison roles have developed over the last 15 or so years, with different names, such as community teacher, teacher keyworker, teacher/social worker etc., with widely differing provision in full and part-time posts and responsibilities. There are many potential and actual pitfalls and it is a very difficult role to fulfil, calling for a rather special blend of personality and experience.

Nevertheless, when it *is* successful, the development of a post of responsibility, in one form or another, can bring an extra dimension to a school's home–school efforts both in directly building bridges between school, family and neighbourhood and in supporting the work of colleagues in this area. More specifically, such a role can facilitate the following points.

WORK WITH FAMILIES

- Initiating and developing contacts with families (especially, perhaps, those who find it most difficult, for one reason or another, to go through the usual channels).
- Encouraging the involvement of parents in the life and work of the school.
- Interpreting the educational needs and interests of children, parents and the local community to the school
- Identifying particular and special needs and appropriate responses.
- Creating broad and varied links with the wider community.

WORK WITH THE SCHOOL AND ITS TEACHERS

- Taking a lead or acting as a catalyst in the development of an effective and wide-ranging home–school programme.
- Providing a picture of the circumstances of local family life for colleagues, based on direct experience not hearsay or folklore.

- Enabling the school to become more responsive to the needs, wishes and experience of families and neighbourhoods.
- Supporting colleagues in their work with families and parents: by sharing experience; by organizing, and contributing to, relevant professional development activities; and by standing in for colleagues, from time to time, so that they can become directly involved themselves.
- Playing a leading part in the evaluation of home–school activity and organizing this as constructive feedback leading to further development.
- Creating the links that enable the school to make more effective use of other agencies with responsibility for, and experience of, the health, education and welfare of children and young people.

As can be seen from these examples, there is considerable scope for overlap and tension between these roles and the allocation of professional responsibility, whatever form they take. Some of these are available by looking at the whole picture in a systematic but flexible way. But others are likely to remain as deep-seated and intractable issues, where success is to reduce tension to a manageable level. People working in home–school liaison roles, for example, are always likely to feel like 'piggy in the middle', pulled in opposite directions by the sometimes contradictory needs of schools and families. In a similar way, the extensive devolution of responsibility to form tutors and class teachers, whilst having great advantages, will also create some new problems which sooner or later will need to be tackled.

Six useful strategies for improving home–school practice

In this section, a number of different lines of development are briefly outlined and illustrated. The different elements should not, however, be thought of as a number of self-contained suggestions to be either randomly selected or slavishly applied in turn. Instead, they should be considered as a number of overlapping, linked elements in a broad approach to the improvement of home–school practice.

All of these elements will need to be looked at as each draws attention to a different aspect of a school's potential efforts in this area. They are unlikely, however, to call for equal commitment, given the changing nature of a school's concerns and priorities.

i) The critical examination of existing arrangements

There can be no better place to begin, for any teacher wishing to improve his or her work with parents, than with an examination of their own existing efforts in this area, together with a wider look at the institution in which they work. Such a process may well be sparked off by a particular problem or event, such as a poor parents' evening or the spread of misleading rumours about the school. Or it might be the gradual acknowledgement that certain things aren't working as well as they should.

Sooner or later, however, it is likely that it will become necessary to carry out a thorough and reasonably systematic examination of the existing arrangements as a whole, in relation to both intentions and actual practice. Such a review, as well a providing a useful picture of the strengths and weaknesses of current arrangements, can often serve as a powerful stimulus to further development and, if the conditions are right, as a catalyst for wider and deeper change. This account is scattered with examples of situations and activities that have served as the starting points for development and change in this way.

In a similar manner, the process of critically examining one's own practice can have different starting points within an institution. It can follow a lead from the head, acting on his or her own initiative or as a response to actual or perceived pressures from 'the outside world' in one form or another; it can originate or develop, from whole staff or departmental meetings, from task groups such as working parties or from meetings of year or class tutors. Finally, it can result from a variety of informal activities and development work, involving varying degrees of individual and collaborative work amongst colleagues.

Such diverse origins have their own strengths and weaknesses, their own characteristic approaches and problems. In the present context, however, emphasis is given to the broader arena, with its focus upon the development of: a 'whole school' approach; the development of agreed home–school policies; and, the planning, organization and evaluation of a broad and wide-ranging programme of practice.

The critical examination of existing arrangements is likely to incorporate four main tasks or functions, though the emphasis upon each may change drastically with rapidly changing needs and circumstances and as a response to very different pressures from other directions (at the time of writing, the imposition of a national curriculum and of testing would be good examples of this).

The critical examination of existing arrangements is required, in one form or another, as part of: (1) a fundamental review and re-appraisal of purposes, policies and practices, from time to time (e.g. as a response to important new legislation, reorganization or the arrival of a new head). (2) The constant monitoring of the home–school programme to ensure its continuing effectiveness, which requires that decisions are taken against a background of evidence and reliable information (e.g. to improve the match between what the parents want and what the school can offer). (3) The need to give attention to particular issues and practices, as these are identified (e.g. low levels of parental involvement, the experience of ethnic minority families etc.). (4) The careful and honest evaluation of new developments in this area (e.g. the annual report and meeting, home-visiting schemes etc.).

For a number of compelling reasons, summarized in the next section, teachers now seem much more willing and able to examine their work in a systematic, self-critical way and to learn from that experience. As a result of this change schools and teachers seem increasingly prepared to borrow from the range of established sources, on a very pragmatic basis and to adapt these to their own needs and circumstances.

Relevant examples are drawn from:

- The use of consumer research techniques to survey parental attitudes and experience, using interviews and questionnaires, suggestion boxes, 'surgeries' etc.
- The use of computing, mapping and other techniques to record and analyse parental attendance, participation and involvement in the home–school programme.

- More frequently, the use of a range of practical techniques for the gathering of evidence drawn from fieldwork research, (previously utilized by curriculum evaluators) suitably adapted to the needs of hard-pressed teachers. These include: participant observation, by individuals and through pairing with a colleague; field notes and tape recordings; different kinds of interviews and group discussions; video recording of both routine and special events; case-studies of selected individuals, groups and/or practices; and analyses of written materials and other forms of documentary evidence.

The important thing about the use of such techniques is not their methodological purity. All will require modification to make them practical and relevant. What really matters is the development of an attitude which sees the need to base policies and judgements on the best available evidence, of whatever kind, as a 'normal' part of the work of schools and teachers.

ii)   *Listening to parents*

It might seem strange that there should be a separate section with this title, since 'listening to parents' has been clearly established as a recurring theme running across the whole of this book, as it has been of the author's work over the last decade or so.

It is useful, I believe, to make a commitment to such a position explicit at least once in an account of this kind, particularly in terms of its practical implications and possibilities. So listening to parents is here seen as a key element in any effective rationale of home–school relations, which has important implications for the development of practice, which are now illustrated.

The willingness to listen to what parents are saying about their children's education and to be responsive to that is an important philosophical stance for teachers, based upon the right of parents, the importance of their support and their value as an educational resource.

Each of these overlapping areas is important and needs to be acknowledged in any worthwhile home–school programme. Listening to parents should be, or should become, an important perspective in the planning, organization and evaluation of home–school activities, incorporating their needs, wishes and experience; providing a crucial ingredient in any worthwhile educational partnership and making them more responsive to the lives of children, families and neighbourhoods.

Listening to parents is not abstract principle or echoing rhetoric, but the basis of a number of practical ideas. A home–school strategy should, therefore, attempt to strengthen existing opportunities to make this possible, develop appropriate new mechanisms together with the necessary professional skills to make it work.

Practical examples include:
- Joint planning groups, parent committees etc, which might tackle a wide variety of suitable tasks according to circumstances and the stage of a school's development, e.g. jointly planning information for the new intake, producing a newsletter or identifying other kinds of joint activities.
- Following up issues, ideas and anxieties raised by parents during the course of teacher–parent interviews. These will be both specific to the

progress of individual pupils and also of a more general nature, such as the value of play or the introduction of GCSE.

- Trying out group parent evenings, using volunteer form tutors or class teachers, to outline the coming term's work (see Chapter 3: Class meetings) to identify concerns and anxieties and, most important, to agree ways in which parents might help.
- Develop a small-scale home-visiting programme with the express purpose of listening to parents on their own territory. This experience might be carefully monitored by a staff working group or other mechanism and a deliberate attempt made to see what can be learned from the experience.
- Planning INSET Days (from the 'Baker 5!') on home–school topics, in which parents will make some contribution.

These are a few, varied examples, drawn from a much wider range of possibilities, of ways in which schools can listen to parents. As such, they will often call for the development not only of new attitudes, but of new forms of organization and new ways of working.

What matters to most parents, however, is not the guarantee of immediate success, but the genuineness of a school's efforts and the spirit in which things are attempted. For parents have often learned, sometimes from painful experience, that schools can sometimes deal in mere window dressing or even devious posturing. As a consequence, many have well-developed antennae for picking up vague do-gooding or half-hearted commitment, the voice that speaks with forked tongue or carefully concealed attempts to manipulate. So be warned – don't do it if you don't mean it!

iii)   Tapping the grapevine

A few years ago it seemed reasonable to think of parents, as a group, being more or less synonymous with the wider community. For, in many neighbourhoods, most households would have had children of school age. In addition, many neighbourhoods were, or were perceived as being, closely-knit communities with widely-shared values and a common lifestyle – a 'Coronation Street' view based on the way people would like things to be more than as the way things were.

This seems a million light years away! Falling birth rates and greater life expectancy mean that, in many neighbourhoods, households with children of school age have become a minority, albeit a large one; housing and redevelopment policies, changes in the economy and the spread of affluence have created massive movements in the population, especially from urban centres to their suburbs; finally, deep and complicated changes have occurred in the ethnic and social composition of many neighbourhoods, changing their nature profoundly. As the cumulative result of such changes, many of the neighbourhoods from which our pupils come, particularly in our larger cities, are rapidly changing and unstable, often characterized by deep divisions and acute tensions, which can readily spill over into open conflict.

If this sounds like an extract from a sociology textbook, I can only apologise! For it is necessary to locate home–school relations against a realistic picture of how communities actually are, not how we think we remember them from our childhood, nor how we would like them to be. For an effective home–school programme cannot put its head in the sand, or deal only in bland solutions. It must, instead, recognize and respond to the needs, wishes and experience of parents and families as they are – warts and all. The following section, then, tries to identify a general approach to such a complex and demanding task and to suggest some practical leads.

Schools wishing to review the effectiveness of their links with their neighbourhoods and the wider community will probably start by attempting to build some kind of picture or profile of the area. This might be based around a framework that looks at:

- Key locations and activities;
- Influential people;
- Main communications networks and styles;
- Important concerns, conflicts and divisions.

In many places, such as a multi-cultural setting, a clear mix of social classes or, say, for a secondary school whose catchment area incorporates sharply contrasting neighbourhoods and communities this would produce a very complex picture. In addition most communities have both formal structures, with official provision and organizations, 'respectable' and legitimate leadership, public resources etc., and, informal structures, deriving from unofficial activity, 'grass-roots' concerns, interests and patterns of organization.

In some communities, the formal and informal structures, cultures and patterns of living overlap considerably: in many, they do not. A school's awareness of these relationships will depend both on the kind and degree of contact it has and also with the extent that it identifies, and works exclusively within, the formal dimension, through its contacts with official organizations, other professionals working in the area etc. Characteristic home–school concerns stemming from this area include the recent history and reputation of the school and the differing expectations that different parents, and groups of parents, currently have of it, also the willingness of the school to adopt a wider community role, rather than limit itself to transmission of testable knowledge, and the capacity of the school to play a unifying role in relation to the diverse needs and experience of its children and their families; the corresponding need to cater for diversity and wide-ranging needs, e.g. special arrangements, materials in different languages and forms etc.

Such profound, complex and intractable issues can never, of course, be resolved on a particular occasion or through specific measures. They are, perhaps, best thought of as part of a continuing attempt, by schools, to strengthen those parts of the home–school programme that can be shown to be working well; to identify problem areas and gaps in provision on a regular basis and tackle them in the light of existing circumstances and resources; and, to pinpoint and work on areas of actual and potential growth and development.

A key strategy, in any work that involves the wider community in which the school is located is tapping the grapevine. The parental grapevine, for example, carries important images and information about the life and work of the school. There may be many different versions of this, which can be very different to how the school sees things, but it is very influential.

If the grapevine appears to be negative or to carry messages that appear to be unfair or untrue, it is because most schools have not been sufficiently aware of its existence, have refused to accept what it is saying about the school and its teachers or have not realized the possibilities for feeding in positive, counter signals and making constructive challenges to the 'bush telegraph'.

Useful tactics here include: the location of some home–school activities in community venues, particularly those in which the parents concerned will feel more at ease; organizing public events and exhibitions, featuring the life and work of local schools, in significant neighbourhood locations, e.g. the health centre, the local chippy etc.; the use of local papers and radio, both for regular information and special features; the sharing of school and community resources of different kinds, with individuals and groups; and, the development of 'outreach' work of different kinds (in the community and on its terms). Good sources of practical ideas in this area are contained in the work of Midwinter, in Liverpool in the 1960s and John Rennie, in Coventry, during the 1970s.

iv)   Engaging in practical activities – especially of a joint nature

It is often more effective in terms of both professional development and the likely success of joint teacher–parent ventures, to get started with a practical task, rather than try to anticipate and resolve beforehand all kinds of foreseeable problems and matters of principle. For deeper issues will inevitably be raised in the carrying out of practical tasks, but in ways that are less likely to sabotage their successful completion. There is also a lot to be said for learning by doing, as we all know, but do not always practise!

In engaging in practical tasks, it is generally easier to see what has been achieved, to be encouraged by this and to become committed to the next stage. This applies every bit as much to teachers as parents!

Practical activities often have an innate flexibility, that is suited to the lives of hard-pressed teachers and parents, that overlong planning and initial discussion don't have. Such activities can, for example, usually be reduced to a manageable scale or level, done in stages, stopped and re-started. They can usually be divided-up between a number of people, whilst retaining much of the value of collaborative activity.

Above all, practical activity, particularly when it can become the object of critical reflection, has been very badly underrated in our society in general and in our education system in particular. Perhaps an example will help. I have worked with teachers in schools on several occasions using video to make a 'visual prospectus' to show the life and work of the school to new parents.

At first, most teachers regard this as a pretty straightforward task, involving the selection and organization of 'information' for parents. In the event, however, such a task often opens up important lines of growth and development stemming from such questions as:

- What does the school believe it is trying to do and what does it actually do?
- What should parents be shown and why?
- What do parents need to know, or are they entitled to know?
- What kinds of relationship do we currently have with our parents?
- How do these come about, and are we happy with them?

Practical tasks: some recent examples

- Designing or updating the school brochure
- Making a video of classroom life to use as the basis for a discussion with parents
- Running a joint teacher–parent newsletter
- Joint projects, based around the school, e.g. converting an unused room into a community room or resource centre
- Producing joint guidelines for parents' evenings
- Trying out exciting innovations on a small-scale, voluntary basis. Examples, developed a little further elsewhere in this book, include: home-visiting; running home–school activities in community venues; family learning sessions; involving pupils in teacher–parent interviews; informal adult education; and class teacher– tutor group parents' evenings.

v)   Establishing home–school matters as a priority in the school's development plan

Recent legislation reinforces the existing LEA requirement for schools to produce their own development plan, outlining current policies and future developments against a wider background of declared national and local priorities. Whilst one might deplore the authoritarian managerial style which has characterized this it remains, with qualification, an important opportunity to make constructive proposals about some important areas of our work in schools and classrooms.

Against this background, the development of more effective thinking and practice in the field of home–school relations can be seen in terms of three linked tasks: (1) getting home–school matters established as a regular item on the professional agendas of schools and teachers, (2) drawing attention to the role of organizational development, to the role of creative management and to the development of appropriate mechanisms for the formulation of policy and the development of good practice, and (3) having an effective school strategy in this area which is focused upon the training needs of teachers and the conditions for their professional development.

The development of such a strategy would be furthered by taking the following practical measures:

- Raising home–school matters at staff meetings
- Setting up a working party/thinktank/study group (preferably including some parents) to report to the staff as a whole at an agreed and suitably realistic time.
- Earmarking a post of special responsibility for a suitable member of staff (equivalent to 0.5 of a teaching post) to develop the school's work in this area. Negotiate the role and its relationship to the existing home–school programme. What price LMS here?
- Encouraging action inquiry approaches, as a means of getting colleagues to look critically at their work.
- Identifying, through honest discussion, the school's training needs in this area and convert these into a systematic programme.

- Enlisting the active support of a knowledgeable and sympathetic outsider, who can combine sharp insight and a knowledge of the issue with 'street credibility' amongst staff.
- Organizing a home–school INSET day (using one of the 'Baker 5' training days allowed to schools).
- Exploiting the GRIST arrangements for the funding of in-service work and the release of teachers. At the time of writing, they appear to offer some unexpectedly good opportunities to harness the provision of inset experiences to the needs of practising teachers in this, and other, areas. They also appear to be responsive to LEAs and schools that are prepared to take some initiatives, rather than wait to see what will be handed down. This, of course, is likely to be a temporary phase, as provision hardens and becomes rationalized, and control over expenditure becomes tighter.

vi) *Borrowing from other people's ideas and experience*

It makes clear sense to me that this section, which opened by asking schools and teachers to begin by examining their own ideas and existing experience, should close by drawing attention to that of other people. Unless this is to be a rather mindless, magpie-type activity, however, with little lasting benefit, there are at least two major areas that require prior consideration.

In the first place, the more a school is able to consider what it is trying to do and look critically at the way it is going about it, the more likely it is to become aware both of its own needs and of the present limitations or resources and experience. This, in turn, will make it more able to locate appropriate ideas and experience to borrow from others.

Secondly, it is almost always the case that borrowed experience will need modification and change before it will fit into a new context. Curriculum development used to talk about the need to 'Adopt and Adapt' or, more homely, the need to 'knock off the corners to get it through the door'! In both causes, effective borrowing from other people requires a capacity to relate other people's experience and circumstances to your own, rather than merely plug holes or use crisis measures.

In this section, a number of very different sources of ideas and experience are identified. They give emphasis to the kind of learning that can follow personal contact with individuals and groups who are actively involved in the home–school field. This should be examined in conjunction with 'Some Useful Sources', with which there is some overlap and which inevitably gives emphasis to a more widely accessible body of recorded experience in different forms.

It is surprising how often teachers are unaware of, or overlook, interesting ideas and experience that are right under their noses, things being done by colleagues with other classes and in other departments. So the most obvious starting point is *at home*, where arrangements are often needed to enable teachers in the same school to pool ideas and share experience.

Although they tend to be unevenly located and distributed, most LEAs have known individuals who are actively involved in the field, who write about it and who know where the interesting developments are currently taking place. Such people, who include LEA advisers, teacher's centre leaders, retired headteachers, tutors in colleges and university departments etc., should also have the kind of first-hand knowledge that enables them to distinguish between exaggerated reputation and solid achievement, which is important in this, as other, educational areas. Key figures may be knowledgeable about and sympathetic to work in this area without necessarily being personally committed or directly involved themselves (see also Section 1, The Role of the LEA).

Taking a wider view, there are still a number of long-term and well-developed home–school projects, in different parts of the country, from which a great deal can be learned, especially from personal visits. Such projects make an invaluable contribution, both in generating new ideas and experience in a concentrated way and also in consolidating more familiar territory.

It is true that such projects are currently tending to keep their heads down, due to their vulnerability to the corporate knives of treasury and finance departments. The sources of funding have also shifted to the EEC, Inner City Partnership, MSC and a few committed LEAs such as Liverpool, ILEA and Humberside in England and Strathclyde and Lothian in Scotland. Such projects include Parents in Partnership, PACT, Homestart, Parent Support Programme, together with a number of smaller projects that can be identified in the CEDC newsletter 'Network', or in the education press generally.

Parent-led organizations have – largely as the result of being obliged to become politicized – more actively pursued their interests in recent years. Long-established bodies such as the National Campaign of PTAs, the Advisory Centre for Education and the Confederation for the Advancement of State Education have, for instance, recently sponsored and commissioned research and studies. Their findings have challenged the complacent or partisan claims of the government and politicians generally, as well as making alternative ideas and experience available to teachers.

In addition, the present government's commitment to consumerism and a market approach to the provision of schooling has led to a number of local pressure groups that are based on particular situations and issues, such as school closures and race conflicts. These raise a number of deep and often intractable home–school issues and are certainly worth investigation. Finally, there is now a diverse and rapidly growing literature, consisting of a wide range of published accounts, based on the thinking and practice of others, which constitute a valuable resource, when handled critically.

Planning an INSET day

A significant feature of the government's dealings with the education service in recent years has been a continuing attempt to formalize both the nature of teachers' responsibilities and their conditions of service. One of the more constructive opportunities opened up by this concern is the 'Baker 5' – the contractual obligation for teachers to allocate five days per year for further training and professional development. Within this quota, a pattern has rapidly become established and widespread, whereby schools can harness their current priorities and concerns to the provision of tailor-made, in-house INSET experiences. Such provision is ideally suited to the development of home–school work in a whole school setting.

In practice, school-based INSET can take a variety of forms and serve a range of purposes. Here, however, such days have been chosen to illustrate a whole school approach, together with some of the possibilities of a single topic focus and of a school's capacity to:

- review its own performance;
- identify its own issues and concerns;
- locate problems to be tackled;
- pinpointing areas of growth and development in the light of its own particular needs, circumstances, experience and resources.

INSET Days can serve a range of purposes, each of which is likely to develop its own characteristics, form and content. This range typically includes:

- Whole school review – perhaps along the lines of the GRIDS Project (Guidelines for Review and Internal Development in Schools) or current LEA leads in the identification of school-based development priorities, e.g. home–school relations; the quality of pastoral care; internal communication.
- 'Consciousness raising' – in complex problematic areas, such as race and gender, where real progress is both long-term and difficult to assess.
- Launching a new project or approach, e.g. involving parents in their children's reading; GCSE etc.
- Tackling a crucial issue in the school's life, e.g. school reorganization; the links between parental choice and falling pupil rolls.
- Consolidating a small-scale or temporary activity – moving it on to a wider base or incorporating it into the mainstream of the life and work of the school, e.g. curriculum innovations, home visiting schemes.

INSET days: preparing the ground

This section sees preparation as a key activity in a process in which planning, organization and evaluation are linked inseparably together, raising a number of issues that, sooner or later, need to be thought through.

An Inset day needs to be considered as both a special event and as part of a process of continuous development. As a special event it offers the opportunity to stop and consider, to give special attention to, to look at things a little differently. On the other hand, unless INSET activity acknowledges the everyday realities of schools and classrooms, it stands little chance of longer term survival, let alone having any lasting effect. The purposes of the day, the selection of its focus and the form it takes need to be grounded in the teachers' own experience and based on the expressed needs of individual teachers, of groups and of the school as a whole. It also needs to seek a reasonable measure of initial support, not only from the head and senior staff, but across the staff, at all levels; and involve colleagues in its planning and organization. The organization of the day's programme should be lively, varied and interesting, utilizing a range of activities and approaches, with opportunities to see, discuss and, above all, experience. It should draw upon previously collected material that relates to the theme, so that the day doesn't start absolutely 'cold', and recognize the existence of important differences of attitude and experience, relevant to the issues concerned. (This is particularly true of issues that bite deeply into the *personal* dimension, such as gender and race, or of differences between staff, as well as between teachers and parents, in the consideration of home–school matters.)

An effective INSET day will leave most staff feeling that the day has been worthwhile and useful in terms of the development of new ideas, attitudes and practices. This is not always easy to pin down, although it is always worth trying to do so. The day's achievements, for example, might not take a tangible form, but be embodied in the kinds of satisfaction expressed during the evaluation of the day's programme; the sowing of important seeds for areas of genuine growth and longer-term development; and the formation of follow-up groups of different kinds to tackle newly identified tasks and issues, to report back at a later stage. At this point, it is important to 'accentuate the positive'!

It is useful to recognize and reinforce the benefits of INSET activity at two levels. First, those that stem from tackling particular topics, issues and problems on a shorter term basis; and secondly, their contribution to curricular, institutional and professional development generally, as part of a cumulative experience and longer term growth and development.

In tackling home–school issues, a special 'X factor' is undoubtedly the 'presence' of parents. This might be true in a literal sense, with the involvement of parents in the planning of the day, as well as their participation in its discussions and activities. It is also true in a figurative sense, in that the views and experience of parents, as a whole, are represented in the work that is undertaken and in the developments that are initiated and pursued.

Some common types of INSET activity and experience

| Lecturers and talks | – keynote speeches |
| | – contributions from outside experts etc. |

| Discussion groups | – different kinds of small groups |
| | – question and answer sessions etc. |

Activity-based	– structured tasks and activities
	– the analysis of educational products
	– simulation and role play etc.

Workshops	– making things 'for real'
	– planning new courses
	– making a video, curriculum materials etc.

Some common faults

1.   Trying to cram too much in

2.   Adopting too broad, or too narrow, a focus

3.   Too much talk - not enough action

4.   Inappropriate contributions from outside experts, or too much reliance upon what they say

5.   Being too idealistic - or too self critical

6.   Playing it too safe

7.   Ignoring, or trying to suppress, important unforeseen events and
        reactions

8.   Failing to make the most of positive reactions and constructive leads

9.   Too much emphasis on the day as a single, self-contained event.

The organizational growth of schools and the professional development of teachers

Although this section necessarily focuses much of its attention upon the organizational development of schools and the professional development of teachers, it can do no better than start with another reminder of the importance of parents and families. For professional development in the field of home–school relations should never stray far from a recognition of the rights and responsibilities of parents and the importance of their support and involvement in their children's educational development.

To do this, in practical terms, it is necessary to focus on the central task of learning to communicate effectively with parents through a wide range of opportunities for contact and involvement – to become more sensitive to the circumstances of their lives and so more responsive to their needs, wishes and experience. Within such a view, it is possible to identify three overlapping and essential areas which, together, constitute the basis of an approach to professional development in this area. First, the development of attitudes and relationships, which grow out of our changing beliefs about families and schools and their place in the wider society. This, in turn, shapes our general intentions and purposes and our expectations of what will, and should, happen in this part of our work. Secondly, the development of appropriate organizational forms and responses, whose functions are widely accepted and clearly understood. These will need to be tailor-made to do the job and this applies just as much to basic arrangements for parental contact as to some of the more imaginative and unusual joint home–school enterprises. Thirdly, the development of effective ways of working towards agreed goals and the means of getting things done, to produce the kind of positive results and experience that can do so much to transform home–school relations.

The conditions for genuine organizational growth and professional development are, of course, both diverse and complex, varying according to the circumstances and experience of schools and teachers. All I can do, in this section is to identify one or two promising areas and possibilities.

To begin with, everyone needs to be clear about what the school is trying to achieve. More than this, however, everybody needs to be involved, in some form or other, in the making of decisions that affect their work in this area. This applies every bit as much to junior colleagues as to well-organized parents. It is an interesting, and not uncommon paradox, that some heads appear happy to pursue a more 'open' policy towards families and the outside world, through an authoritarian stance in the staffroom!

A broad and varied home–school programme needs the development of considerable management skills, to bring about the planning, organization and evaluation of the wide range of activities that this entails. It calls for leadership (not always from the top and not always from the school side) to provide a wider perspective and a longer-term view, to create a sense of shared purpose and the conditions for its realization. It calls for the capacity to coordinate a range of efforts, to facilitate the maintenance of existing activities and to support the emergence of new ones. Above all, it calls for skill to recognize and resolve the tensions and difficulties that are the inevitable result of differences of perspective and experience between teachers, pupils and parents.

These are formidable tasks for which a wide range of solutions and approaches are continually being canvassed in the educational press and in the training and professional development of teachers. Here, I would like to draw attention briefly to two possibilities.

A pattern of school organization, which is sometimes called 'collegial' and which has the following characteristics:

- A flexible, relatively non-hierarchical structure and staffing. In particular, ideas are valued for their own merit, not according to the seniority of the person they come from.
- A collaborative approach to its major tasks, where sharing and joint activity is regarded as the normal way of going about things.
- The use of negotiation as a key element in planning, decision-making and the resolution of problems.
- A broad, rather than a narrow, view of education which recognizes both its wider implications and its longer-term effects.
- A task-centred approach, with a strong desire to get on with the main business, rather than waste time and energy in peripheral distractions.
- Above all, the capacity of the institution and those who work in it and with it, to try to improve their work and to learn from attempts to do so.

The move towards a 'collegial approach' and to a more open and flexible institution, is well-suited to the development of more effective home–school relations. It should not, however, be seen as the movement from one fixed structure to another. For it is more akin to a process of development which is appropriate not only to this, but to other, different but also important, contemporary educational tasks.

The second line of approach, ironically, owes something to the politician's drive towards improving the quality of the teaching profession, made possible by the contraction of the education service, which has served as a catalyst to a number of changes that are already taking place. For a long time now, teachers have shown an increasing willingness to examine their own work critically, both individually and with colleagues, to work within agreed policies and planned programmes, to look for evidence of the effectiveness of their work, and to see the need for engaging in continuing development and change, through the adoption of appropriate strategies and techniques. As a consequence, considerable emphasis has been given to in-service activity that can be partly located on-site, is school-focused and grows readily out of the basic, everyday work of teachers.

More recently, this has been accelerated by the funding arrangements for INSET and teacher release (Grant Related In-Service Training [GRIST]), which has given a considerable boost to 'action-inquiry' approaches, whose overall aim is the development of more effective practice.

Such approaches seem to have much to offer to the thoughtful practitioner in the home–school field. For they provide a framework and a process through which the concerns of hard-pressed teachers and the anxieties and frustrations of parents can be examined in a critical, but constructive, way. For action-inquiry is built upon an underlying sympathy for the problems that teachers and parents face in their everyday lives. It requires access to the sharply observed realities of the school gate, the corridor and the classroom, to the voices of parents and to the experiences that they express. An action inquiry approach which combines, in varying ways, the investigation of a teacher's own practice, structured reflection upon it and the development of practical initiatives, has a number of important advantages within a whole school approach. Such an approach makes individual schools (and teachers within them) the focal point of their own development, in terms of both responsibility and action; it makes existing practice the starting point; gives greater emphasis to the need to combine thinking and practice, through the critical analysis of one's own work; allows plenty of scope to tap into parental perspectives and experience, as well as professional ones; allows access to the 'wider view' and outside experience (e.g. of 'experts') on the school's own terms and when it is ready to do so; is based upon a view of change as continuous development, rather than as a series of one-off 'events'; and, above all, action research and inquiry requires an investigative spirit, a willingness to examine existing policy and practice, and to think it through in ways that suggest and pinpoint areas of growth and further development. Such approaches, which are substantially represented in both the organization and contents of this collection, have a valuable contribution to make to both the study and practice of family–school relations.

So a collegial pattern of organization, which encourages collaboration and the sharing of ideas and experience and action inquiry approaches, which stress the self critical examination of one's own work, whilst not new in themselves, typify a developing professionalism amongst teachers. Such an approach seems to be very much in tune with our times, its major concerns and preoccupations.

3 The Development of More Effective Practice

The development of a whole programme – from planning to evaluation

This section is built around a more down-to-earth version of a very basic model of planned change which stresses the relationships between educational intentions, processes and outcomes. It does so by combining two different kinds of emphasis. First, the general concerns stem from the application of such a model almost anywhere in the educational system, to, for instance, planning issues, or the links between basic beliefs and organizational forms or to the relationships between planning and evaluation. Secondly, we look at the special concerns of this book and the corresponding emphasis upon the series theme of *Parents and Teachers*, which examines how far, and in what ways, the perspectives and experience of parents are acknowledged by schools, and, even better, incorporated into subsequent plans and arrangements for home–school activities and their evaluation; and the development of a whole school approach and its broad concern with home–school thinking and practice as a whole (Figure 3.1).

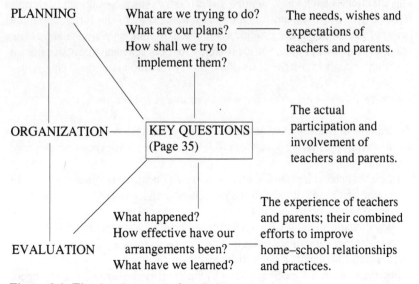

PLANNING   What are we trying to do?   The needs, wishes and
                        What are our plans? —— expectations of
                        How shall we try to   teachers and parents.
                          implement them?

                                           The actual
ORGANIZATION——— | KEY QUESTIONS | —— participation and
                          (Page 35)   involvement of
                                      teachers and parents.

                                       The experience of teachers
             What happened?   and parents; their combined
             How effective have our   efforts to improve
EVALUATION   arrangements been?—— home–school relationships
             What have we learned? and practices.

Figure 3.1: The development of a whole programme

Although teachers are being asked to produce plans, schemes of work and so on, that cover more and more of their work in schools, and in spite of the obvious value of much genuine planning, fundamental attitudes towards educational planning remain a mixture of cynical amusement, deep mistrust and healthy scepticism. In particular, there seem to be three areas of suspicion. First, that planning is not very real – sometimes teachers are asked to produce plans that no one has any intention of implementing. As a result they sometimes read more like a fantasy journey than a guide for action in the real world. Realistic plans need to be rooted in the kinds of planning which teachers *do* make and find useful as part of their work. Secondly, that planning is not always helpful – in particular, it is hard to strike a balance between planned activity and spontaneous response. If, for example, plans are too rigidly conceived, or slavishly followed, they are counter-productive, making things boring, predictable and lifeless. While having some sympathy for such a view, it is fairly easy to parody or caricature. Thirdly, you can't start with a clean slate – some kinds of planning have a drawing-board quality about them. The development of more effective home–school relations, in particular, even given the catalyst of important changes of legislation or of key personnel, has to acknowledge a number of pre-existing features and circumstances, attitudes and practices, such as:

- the contextual features of school and neighbourhood;
- existing arrangements for home–school contact;
- the present attitudes and experience of schools and families, of teachers, pupils and parents respectively; and build these into their planning, organization and evaluation.

Planning and evaluation are, in important ways, two sides of the same coin, although the relationship is often somewhat obscure and undervalued. For a broad plan can clarify our intentions, enable us to establish priorities, identify how we set about realizing them, and help us to anticipate some of the obstacles and problems that are likely to be encountered. Evaluation, on the other hand requires us to find out what has actually taken place and relate this to our original intentions, enables us to improve our efforts next time, and makes it possible to learn from our experience in a more systematic way. The formulation of a series of key questions can provide a useful tool for linking planning and evaluation. It can also draw attention to possible gaps between ideas and actions. Such questions can also form the basis of a critical evaluation later on (Table 3.1).

Planning a home–school programme: aims and purposes

Teachers with whom I have worked over the years have found Figure 3.2 useful in providing a starting point from which to explore the idea of a home–school programme.

In the first place, it provides a framework within which teachers can identify the nature and range of existing home–school activity in their own schools. It is surprising how often teachers will say afterwards, 'I hadn't realized it, but we already do quite a bit!' It is also possible, especially in secondary schools, to be ignorant or lose sight of activities that may be going on elsewhere in the school, from which colleagues might borrow and learn.

Secondly, such a framework serves as a clear reminder that home–school links can serve a very broad range of purposes, incorporating very different

Table 3.1: Planning and evaluating home–school programmes: some questions to consider

Aims and objectives

What are the basic aims of our home–school programme?

Are the general aims sufficiently clear? Are they too general and too vague?

Are the objectives too detailed and too cluttered?

Do our aims and objectives make sense to parents?

How do we know? Do they interpret them in much the same way as we do?

How do we begin to work towards each of our main aims?

What are our priorities?

Scope and range

How broad or limited is our programme?

How far does it acknowledge common interests and problems?

Is it reasonable to talk about 'the parents' view'? Are there different views?

Is there any definite pattern of development in our programme?

Are there special groups who need to be considered separately? These would include working class families in a predominantly middle-class area and vice versa, fathers, shift workers, one-parent families, ethnic groups, etc.

What special provision is required for such groups?

How far does our programme reach, and involve, parents *as a whole?*

Form and style

How is our picture of parents obtained?

What assumptions do we make about their interest, knowledge and skills? How can we make this picture deeper and more accurate?

How varied and wide-ranging is our home–school programme? In particular do we give enough emphasis to informal contact and activity, and to positive and personal situations?

How do the different views that parents have influence our work?

Strategies and tactics

What are the points of growth in our programme?

As well as a short-term policy, do we also have a longer-term view of where we are going?

Are we going - too quickly to consolidate thoughtful improvement?

- not quickly enough?

How realistic and appropriate is our programme?

Have we done enough preparatory work in terms of:

- staff discussion

- discussion with parents

- identification of resources, support, etc.

In what ways have our attitudes to home–school cooperation changed in recent years:– collectively, as a staff?

– as individuals on the staff?

Evaluation and development

What do parents think about our home–school programme?

How effective, useful and interesting do they find the different elements? How can we improve the 'feedback' that we get from parents?

Are there areas where parents and teachers see things differently?

In what main ways have our efforts improved and developed in recent years?

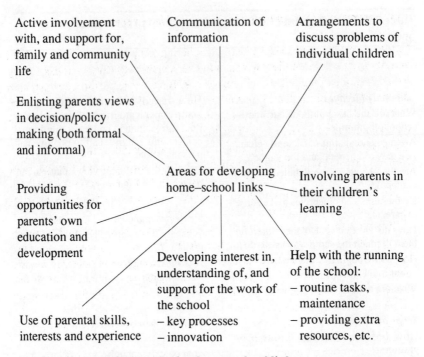

Active involvement with, and support for, family and community life

Enlisting parents views in decision/policy making (both formal and informal)

Providing opportunities for parents' own education and development

Use of parental skills, interests and experience

Communication of information

Areas for developing home–school links

Developing interest in, understanding of, and support for the work of the school
– key processes
– innovation

Arrangements to discuss problems of individual children

Involving parents in their children's learning

Help with the running of the school:
– routine tasks, maintenance
– providing extra resources, etc.

Figure 3.2: Areas for developing home–school links

views about the role of schools in their communities. For teachers and parents have widely-differing, sometimes contradictory views about how far they should go in the sharing of both responsibility and effort. Some teachers, for example, speak as if 'education' in the school and family settings is virtually indivisible; others see a clear demarcation between the two. Both attitudes exist in most staffrooms! Figure 3.2 reveals, in its uncovering of the relationship between purposes and practices, whether a school appears to put its energies into the endorsement of a more limited view of contact based around children's work in classrooms or whether it regards the active support of families as a necessary part of its work as a caring, as well as a learning community.

Thirdly, the diagram serves to remind us of the relationship between purpose and form. The same practice can be used to achieve different means. So, for instance, home visits can be used as a way of getting to know new pupils and their families. More frequently it is a crisis measure used in the management of difficult children.

Finally, such a diagram provides a simple framework with which to start evaluating home–school thinking and practice. As such, it offers an antidote to the kinds of pressure created by everyday life in schools that result in ad-hoc arrangements and an obsessive concern with short term survival. It can offer, instead, a chance to look at the impact of the home–school programme as a whole, identify ideas that are strong and well-developed, as well as the corresponding gaps and weaknesses that need to be tackled and, when this has been done, to pinpoint areas of actual and potential growth and development.

How parents make judgements about their children's schooling

In the preceding pages, I have been considering the planning of home–school activity from a point of view which, however sensitive to parents, is essentially located within an organizational framework. Here, by deliberate contrast, I am offering a sharp reminder, illustrated by the voices of real parents, that all these efforts will be wasted unless schools recognize not only that parents have distinctive needs and anxieties, but also their own ways of tackling them.

For a long time, no one had really thought it important to find out how parents set about the task of making judgements about their children's progress, or lack of it, at school. In recent years, however, a number of efforts have been made, for different reasons, to do just this and to see whether there are any practical lessons to be learned from such an experience.

Even a cursory glance at the following quotations, drawn from our parent interviews, reveals a very complex picture. Something of the flavour of this is uncovered by a brief look at types of information and evidence about pupil's work, behaviour and educational progress; the ways in which parents seek, handle and interpret such evidence; and the access and opportunities that different schools provide for parents to pursue these matters.

Can . . . I ask you how you got a picture of the progress your children were making at this stage?

Mother: I think by a combination of looking at what they were bringing home, and, erm, talking to the teachers and looking at what they had been doing during the term, uh, on the open days.

Father: And seeing what things they did. If they read books at a certain age or they didn't have to be chivvied into reading books. You know, they could clearly add up money.

———————

When you went did you get a chance to look at your children's work?

Father: Yes.

Did you find *that* useful?

Father: Uh, yes and no, because I've got no idea, still haven't really, of the kind of level they should be achieving at that age. The only way you could do it was by putting a lot of work out to compare it with, and by going and looking at your kid's books and by going and looking at the other children's work, you'd get a comparison of how they stood in the same sort of period.

Mother: You know you can tell by the books how many rights, how many wrongs there are, how they're doing and you know, OK.

———————

Mother: Yes, I do, because all the bookwork that they work with they keep in a box. So if you're early, or even if the teacher's running late you can sit and look through your child's work and take in comments what the teacher's written. So you've got a rough idea how they're going on in maths, English and other subjects by looking at the books, seeing what work they're doing and teachers'comments in them. Whereas, on the senior side, you don't see any of the books, you know you're just reading, they do like a report on ya.

———————

Father: If it's a good written report that's almost enough. But if it's, "Could do better" or "Satisfactory" or something of the sort, then clearly its helpful to chat as well.

Mother: You have to rely on the teacher's judgement plus a little bit of your own when she occasionally does a little bit of homework I want her to do, something you can make some kind of judgement over. You have to rely on the teacher and looking at the child's written work.
. . . but I hadn't really anything to ask him about Sarah's progress because I felt that the school report and her enjoyment of the subject and looking at her books had answered my questions anyway.
What kinds of things do you look for to make your mind up about Claire's maths?

Mother: Well one thing I think is, the younger child, Tim, is a very bright child and when we realize the things that he knows and he can answer the questions and she can't being two years older than him. So it makes you think 'Well is it because he's that much brighter or, you know, because she's lagging behind?' And that's one of the comparisons.
And that's a fairly reliable guide is it, that kind of comparison?

Father: Well, it's the only comparison I've got. You know, I can't compare her with the other kids in the class because I never meet them.

Mother: . . . if you know your child, you can see, you can just *tell* how they're getting on by their . . . it's difficult . . . you can tell by their manner, their attitude, how they look when they walk in the door, the way they talk about school . . . I mean mine have always come, uh, singing and always full of what they've done and always very happy and being very eager . . .
. . . Yes, I think I would know, when my children came home if something had gone wrong . . . if their head was hanging and they looked miserable, I'd immediately think something had gone wrong, then try to find out what it was.

Types of information and evidence

In trying to get to grips with their children's progress, parents have recourse to a wide range and variety of information and evidence, as Figure 3.3 shows clearly. Within this range, however, different parents will have their own preferences, as well as opportunities, to collect relevant and appropriate data. Although it is very difficult to pinpoint these preferences with great accuracy, in our work we have noted a general preference for the following:

- Examining children's work, for themselves
- Talking with teachers (providing that it is a two-way discussion)
- Listening to children's own accounts of school work and life
- Observing the demeanour and motivation of their children towards school activities

Interestingly enough, in spite of the media stereotype of the 'actively concerned parent', most of them do not attach too much importance to marks and grades, finding them impossible to interpret in isolation.

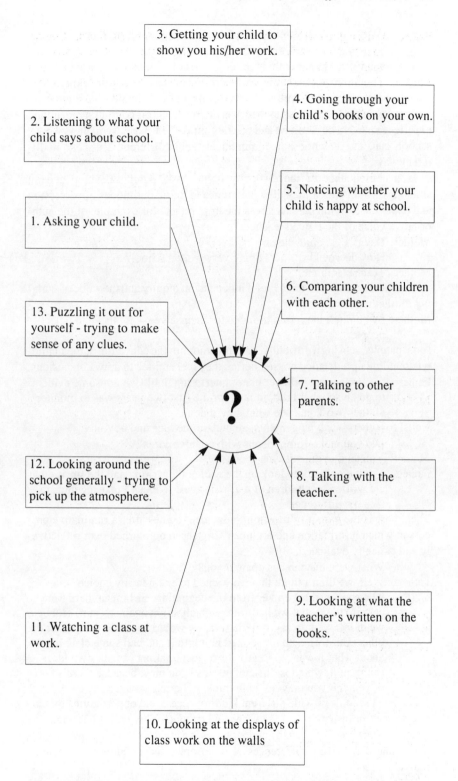

Figure 3.3: How do *you* decide on *your* child's progress?

Ways in which parents seek, handle and interpret evidence

In making judgements about their children's schooling, parents learn that such a process is seldom easy or straightforward. Various messages and experiences have to be checked out; contradictory signals and information have to be set against one another and fresh evidence is often called for; conflicting ideas and experience need to be resolved and puzzles unravelled. To make matters worse, schools can, and do, choose to communicate about different issues and in different ways.

As a consequence of the difficulty of the task, parents develop general strategies within which they give preference to particular modes of perception and experience. Some parents stress the importance, for example, of the authoritative voice of the trained teacher,

Mother: David's . . . quite clever.
How do you know he's doing very well at school?
Mother: Teacher told me.
while others emphasize their belief if independent inquiry and the value of 'judging for themselves';
Mother: I would tell them first to judge for themselves – not listen to other people.
some parents, sensing a difficulty, patiently monitor the education of their children, building up a detailed dossier before they feel entitled to draw conclusions;
Father: . . . I'm a great believer in not interfering until I've got some evidence to go on so what I did, in fact, for the first two years was to monitor all their work and see what they'd done.
whilst for others, such judgements are both immediate and obvious.
Did you make comparisons with other children?
Mother: You tend to do, with his friends.
Father: You've only got to look on the wall at the writing and the stories that are written by children of the same ages. It doesn't take a genius to spot the difference.
Then there is the parent from whom judgement comes after a ruminative process in which information and argument are teased out, turned over reflectively and patiently evaluated.
What were the choices open to you?
Father: Well, we didn't think that we wanted to exclude any choice whatsoever (mm) erm er from the beginning. Er I mean there were certain things that we had were an inclination against, (mm) er, but we didn't want to say well that, er, we would never do this that or the other. Until we actually looked in it into it and had some clear idea about what it was . . . Really it was just thinking out our own ideas (mm) on it, which is difficult because you may, because there's two of you and you may not both think in the same way.

Different schools provide different kinds of access and opportunities for parents to seek information and feed their judgements. This will reflect both the general differences between the major phases in a child's schooling and the variations that derive from differences of philosophy and circumstance between individual schools.

Primary and secondary schools tend to develop their own distinctive patterns of home–school contact, which reflect their respective concerns and patterns of organization. So, for example, primary schools are more likely to make pupils' work available for inspection or to involve parents in classrooms. Secondary schools, by contrast, give greater emphasis to formal arrangements and to marks, grades and written reports, whether or not this meshes in with parental needs (see also Chapter 4 for other implications of the differences between primary and secondary schools).

In a similar way, schools vary from one to another in the seriousness with which they tackle the job not merely of informing parents beyond the legal requirements, but in their willingness to help parents to understand and to become part of an active educational partnership. Sometimes, too, schools, seen from a parent's eye-view, are not nearly as open and forthcoming as they think they are!

Some practical implications

The most effective response is one in which individual schools adapt what they learn to their own particular philosophy, circumstances and stage of development. However, a number of possibilities emerge, because against such a view, the efforts of most schools can seem unnecessarily crude, narrow and restricted. There is generally far too much reliance upon the written word, on one-way teacher dominated talk and, in the secondary school, on personal grades and formal assessment.

By contrast, acknowledging parents' needs suggests the following possibilities.
- Using displays of children's work in schools, libraries and other public venues, perhaps linked with a lively, explanatory leaflet.
- Using pupils to demonstrate and explain aspects of their work to their parents.
- Setting-up special demonstrations and participatory workshops.
- Communicating about things that are taken for granted by teachers, but puzzling to parents, e.g. marking policies.
- Putting together a folder of children's work, with comments, for parents to examine at home. (It seems absolutely amazing to me that some schools actively forbid children to take work home!)
- Informal group discussions with parents, to discuss issues of general concern.
- Running special 'one-offs', to tackle issues of concern that are picked up from the 'parental grapevine' (p. 22).

The different needs of schools and families

Striking a balance: Hoffnung's Barrels

The main argument of this section has been that the plans that schools make in the home–school field, and the practices that result from them, are shaped far too much by school goals and policies, and by teacher needs and ways of doing things. To become more effective, schools need to tune in more to the needs, expectations and experience of parents and families.

Figure 3.4 identifies, in a diagrammatic summary, a number of areas where a different kind of relationship between the goals of schools and the needs of parents needs to be tried out. The metaphor of 'Hoffnung's Barrels' is based on a classic comic sketch, describing the futile efforts of a man on a building site, using a series of pulleys to move heavy objects. As one side is raised, the other

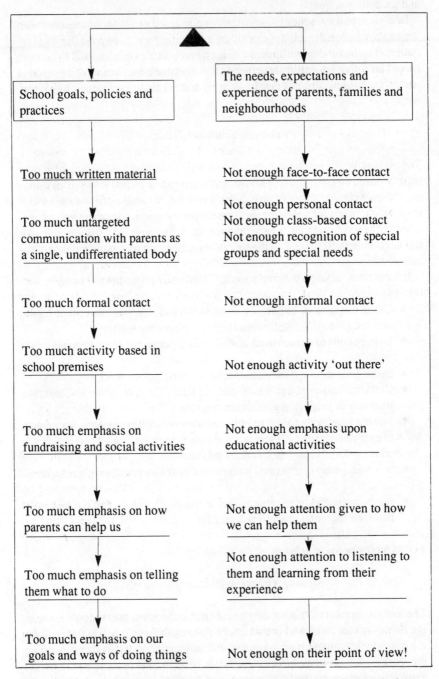

Figure 3.4: The 'Hoffnung's Barrels' approach to home–school relations

ఞ correspondingly falls! As such, it seems appropriate to an attempt to strike a new balance in home–school matters.

The problem of organization

In this section as a whole most of the attention is given to matters that concern planning and evaluation; the organization of home–school activities takes a back seat. The reason for such treatment has nothing to do with the relative import- ance of these areas – quite the reverse! For the organization of a school's efforts and the specialization of ideas is both a recurring theme running throughout this book and also the object of special attention at particular points in it.

It is, for example, a key element in Chapter 2 which deals extensively with the organization and management of home–school relations in a whole school setting. It can also be seen in a number of detailed illustrations of how to or- ganize specific home–school events and activities, see 'Running a curriculum evening' (p. 86) and 'Planning an INSET day' (p. 27). So a strong interest in the development of effective and appropriate organization – in translating ideas into practical forms of action – is never far away.

In the present context, however, the focus is upon organization as a way of raising a number of specific issues. The capacity to develop effective forms of organization and see them implemented is not something that can be taken for granted or merely learned incidentally from growing experience. Like other aspects of professional development, it can only benefit from being undertaken in a systematic and deliberate way, and in relation to thoughtful planning and careful evaluation.

Another fallacy about the organization of practical matters is the assumption that their arrangement is simply a means to an end, neutral in intent and effects and relatively unproblematic. The present account, by contrast, stresses the ex- tent to which the nature, range and scope of home–school activities are shaped by the underlying attitudes and values of those who implement them. This ap- plies equally to the programme as a whole and the extent to which it reinforces breadth or narrowness of purpose, underscores particular priorities and endor- ses a one or two-way flow of information and ideas; and the particular forms of practice which embody, both in content and form, the attitudes and values of those who organize them. Whilst this is generally true, the present account has unearthed a number of examples of common practices that would repay examination in this way, such as school letters routinely sent to parents, teacher- parent interviews (Parents' evenings), curriculum evenings, and arrangements for parents to visit without a prior appointment etc.

The range, scope and variety of home–school links

The development of practical experience in recent years has been spearheaded by the pioneering efforts of teachers and parents in individual schools, rather than as a response to the initiatives of politicians and administrators.

Whilst there has been enormous variation in purpose, commitment and ap- proach between schools, certain general patterns are becoming visible. Home– school arrangements have steadily broadened to reflect a wider range of purposes and a greater repertoire of practice. This also suggests (though I've no means of proving it) that home–school work is being more widely seen as a legitimate obligation and a worthwhile commitment, as opposed to paying lip-service or indulging in empty rhetoric as has often happened in the past. I even believe, in rash moments, that the bonds between many families and their children's schools are stronger as a result of the long-running disputes with the government and because of its current attempts to impose its 'reforms' without any real discussion. Home–school activity seems to have become more concerned with the educational life of the school as its central focus and preoccupation. Fund-raising, social and other supportive activities continue, of course, to be important activities (in many cases literally holding the school up). But they do not have the same significance and interest to those who become involved. The *style* of much home–school contact is slowly changing. There is less reliance upon large-scale meetings and formal presentations, more upon informal, task-orientated, group activities. The emergence of class–tutor group activities is an interesting case in point. Perhaps teachers are transferring the lessons they have learned from their own INSET experiences here.

The boundaries between teaching and parenting, between informal education and formal schooling, do not seem as clear cut as they may have done earlier. Consider the impact of the media or computers upon the lives of children, for example. An important consequence of such wider changes is that teachers (and parents, too) are less likely to consider the education of children and parental development as separate, competing activities, but as linked in important ways.

The following examples have been chosen as representative of a widening repertoire of home–school practice. It is not meant to be comprehensive or definitive, for home–school practice is infinitely diverse and varied. It is, however, a selection which tries to convey something of the range of key forms within a broad view. Because of this, readers will react in very different ways both to the range and to individual examples according to what they think is both legitimate and relevant for them.

Key forms in a basic home–school programme

ARRANGEMENTS FOR GETTING TO KNOW NEW FAMILIES

Face to face meetings, home visits
Giving information, making practical arrangements, establishing relationships.

REGULAR AND CONTINUING INFORMATION ABOUT THE LIFE AND WORK OF THE SCHOOL
Newsletters
Class or tutor group meetings
'Surgeries'
Special events.

INVITATIONS TO COME AND SEE THE SCHOOL AT WORK

Normal routines, e.g. parent assemblies, open classrooms
Special occasions, e.g. concerts, open days, exhibitions.

OPPORTUNITIES TO REVIEW THE PROGRESS OF INDIVIDUAL CHILDREN, AND TO DISCUSS THIS WITH APPROPRIATE TEACHERS

Incorporating examination of children's work, e.g. parent folders, pupil diaries
Both regular formal appointments and ad hoc visits when problems develop, e.g. parents evenings, surgeries
Specially arranged 'case conferences' involving both parents and other relevant professionals.

SUPPORT FOR 'SPECIAL NEEDS' PUPILS, REMEDIAL PROVISION IN SCHOOL AND AT HOME

Co-tutoring arrangements
Negotiated support activities.

HOME VISITS

To get to know a new family
Following up specific concerns
As a response to the failure of previous attempts to establish contact through normal channels of communication
To set up home-based projects and schemes.

UTILIZATION OF PARENTAL HELP AND SUPPORT

Alongside teachers in classrooms
Around the school, e.g. library, resource centre, school bookshop
Working with individuals or small groups
Tapping parental knowledge and skill.

THE INVOLVEMENT OF PUPILS IN THE HOME–SCHOOL PROGRAMME

In curriculum sessions with parents
To actively complete the teacher–parent–pupil triangle at meetings to review progress and within the reporting system.

CURRICULUM EVENINGS IN A VARIETY OF FORMS

With focus on areas of parental anxiety and concern, e.g. maths, topic work, drug education
As an introduction of new subject matter, teaching methods and assessment, e.g. environmental studies, GCSE
As a way of enlisting the active help and support of parents, e.g. for children's reading and language work.

FAMILY SESSIONS HELD IN SCHOOL

To provide opportunities to jointly tackle school-related activities, e.g. maths
and computer work, engineering, creative arts
As a platform for the development, on a family basis, of leisure and recreational
interests and activities, on a less formal basis than is usually the case.

JOINT PARENT–TEACHER ACTIVITIES

Through the PTA (or its equivalents)
As both regular and one-off events and activities, formal and informal.

PARENT CLASSES AND GROUPS THAT ARE A RESPONSE TO BOTH SCHOOL AND
PARENT INITIATIVES

Mums' groups or mums and toddlers' groups
Parent study and support groups, e.g. WEA, Open University or Social Services
sponsored activities
'Positive health' or Keep Fit' classes and activities.

OPPORTUNITIES TO JOIN 'SHARED DAYTIME CLASSES' FOR STUDENTS OF ALL
TYPES AND AGES WHERE APPROPRIATE

Academic and practical classes
Formal and informal adult education, offering different kinds of commitment.

THE IDENTIFICATION OF SPECIAL NEEDS AMONGST PARENTS AND THE DEVELOP-
MENT OF APPROPRIATE RESPONSES AND SPECIAL PROVISION

The need for special kinds of family support
The needs of ethnic minorities
The particular needs of shift workers, single parent families.

THE PROVISION OF 'OUTREACH' WORK

To widen parental participation and involvement
To operate in community settings, where these make the activity more effective.

FORMAL REPRESENTATION AND INVOLVEMENT IN THE MANAGEMENT OF THE
SCHOOL

As an elected member on a representative parent body, e.g. PTA, home–school
council, community council, local CASE group
As a parent governor.

Evaluating home–school thinking and practice

In recent years, evaluation has moved from the position of a rather esoteric exercise grafted on to educational innovations, to an essential feature of any credible curriculum and professional development strategy. Like any such approach, it is likely to be more effective when it has been thought through and adapted to the users' own needs and circumstances - in short, when it becomes a 'natural' and 'normal' part of their way of doing things.

Evaluation is an important means of: showing what has taken place – showing what it has been like for those involved and for those who have a right to know. Teachers and others involved in the education service increasingly accept the right of parents to know what goes on in our schools. The evaluation of home – school relations by teachers shows everyone that it is taking this area of its work seriously, by subjecting it to careful scrutiny and critical examination. To do so indicates an acceptance of professional responsibility and a growing confidence in these matters.

Evaluation also enables a balanced judgement to be made, based on information about what has been attempted and what achieved. At the heart of evaluation lies the relationship between ends and means. For judgements about the effectiveness of home–school programmes and practices must always be related to questions about their value: what we achieve only makes real sense (both to others and to ourselves) in relation to what we have set out to do.

Evaluation provides an important means of bringing ideals and realities into a critical but productive relationship, by matching up claims and actual experience, exposing inconsistencies, discrepancies and contradictions between the two. In the field of home–school relations, fine rhetoric is not always matched by effective action – far from it! So, evaluation helps to provide both a rationale and a method with which teachers can examine their own work. It entails the discussion of purposes, followed by the collection and interpretation of appropriate information and data. This, in turn provides the basis for making more reasonable decisions about policy and practice and for subsequent judgements about their quality. This can be applied equally to the programme as a whole or to the examination of particular practices' as well as uncovering areas legitimate more recent developments.

Evaluation helps the identification of areas of improvement for the future. Evaluation can often offer a guide to more effective action by revealing shared purposes and concerns (not only between teachers and parents, but amongst teachers too) as well as pinpointing areas of difference and disagreement. The more accurately this is done, the more likely it is to suggest practical improvements, as well as areas of potential growth.

Evaluation is also a means of uncovering what has been learned from the experience, for everyone, in ways that can be related to the development of new attitudes and new ways of working. Evaluation is here considered to be very useful as an applied activity which requires the bringing together of ideals and realities and the integration of thinking and practice, as well as the cornerstone of a process which requires teachers to examine critically their own work, as the basis of their professional development.

So evaluation is portrayed here not as a form of externally imposed inter-
ference in the work of schools and teachers, but as a means of understanding
and coming to terms with their present work and as a source of ideas for its future development.

Evaluation is more likely to be effective when it is undertaken for the 'right'
reasons. There are many, often convincing, reasons for doing things in school
– to keep the peace and avoid conflict, to keep others happy, to impress or be
trendy, to gain official support, to put on the c.v. and so on – but the best reason for evaluating home–school activity lies in its positive potential contribution to improvement, development and change, by working towards a
programme of activities that is more genuinely responsive to the needs and experience of parents, teachers and pupils respectively.

Evaluation also tries to strike a balance between competing ideas and contradictory demands. It should, for example, be thorough without becoming too
time-consuming or intrusive: it should divide its time and energy between a consideration of the whole programme and of broader concerns, with the examination of particular issues, problems and forms of contact; it should take into
account the many other, often powerful demands that are being made upon
schools and teachers.

Above all evaluation achieves a sense of overall perspective. Evaluation, by
nature, probes and examines, reveals gaps, discrepancies and weaknesses. It is
all too easy to produce a picture in which ordinary, everyday achievements are
under-reported and undervalued and the critical perspective given too much pro-
minence. It is this essential lack of proportion and overall perspective that makes
many teachers justifiably suspicious of systematic evaluation and leads them to
say, of many final reports, 'Nothing you say is untrue, but it doesn't *feel* right!'
Unless evaluation is convincing in this way it is unlikely to be taken seriously
or to contribute to longer term development.

Some areas needing special emphasis

The evaluation of home–school matters, as well as showing similarities with
other aspects of educational processes, also has its own distinctive features and
problems. These revolve around the declared aims and intentions of the home–
school programme. Here the links between planning and evaluation come home
to roost! For without a clear framework of shared intentions, evaluation is little
more than a shallow, ritualistic activity, undertaken for spurious reasons and un-
connected to longer term development.

This account has suggested a number of frameworks and techniques for exam-
ining actual practice in relation to declared intentions, such as:
- Key questions on the major areas (p. 35)
- The range, scope and variety of home–school links (p. 43)
- Special events: key moments (p. 96)
- Whole programme: special priorities and particular practices, etc. (p. 44)

Another feature is the differing perspectives and experience of teachers,
parents and pupils. In addition to mapping out wavelength differences, in ways
that are illustrated throughout this account, relatively systematic evaluation is
helpful in identifying special needs such as the needs and wishes of parents and

pupils, as opposed to teachers; or, the needs of parents as a whole and also those of particular groups, e.g. ethnic minorities, one parent families with small children or families containing children with disabilities.

The collection of a range of appropriate kinds of information and evidence is an important feature in the evaluation of home–school matters. The following illustration, for example, has been put together (with the permission of the authors of the original report) from the Belfield Reading Project, a school-focused development to monitor the effects of parental involvement in, and support for, their children's reading in a community primary school in Rochdale. It draws upon: both immediate reactions and more considered statements; the views and experience of parents and teachers respectively; the careful use of more systematic records of pupil achievement; and special, home-made materials and approaches, such as the weekly report for parents to fill in.

The evaluation of home–school activity is essentially practical in nature. To be effective, such evaluation needs to be able to develop the ability both to take advantage of opportunities as they arise and to find ways of gathering information and tapping experiences, that are appropriate to individual schools and their communities. Above all, however, a climate needs to be established in which such activities come to be regarded as both natural and essential, for teachers and parents alike.

Evaluating home–school activity: some practical suggestions

In this section, several lines of activity are suggested, not in a definitive 'hints and tips' manner, but as several useful focal points or lines of development, together with a number of suggestions and illustrations for each. The first focuses upon the relationship between general intentions and effective practice. The second identifies several useful mechanisms for a progressive programme of evaluative activity, while the third briefly outlines an approach to the development of effective methods and techniques.

i) THE RELATIONSHIP BETWEEN AIMS, INTENTIONS AND EFFECTIVE PRACTICE

Frameworks that facilitate an examination of the relationship between policies and practices, between words and actions include:
- the formulation of a series of key questions that can be used as the basis of both the planning and evaluation of home–school activity
- the systematic comparison, in turn, of the different views and experience of parents, teachers and pupils respectively
- the use of 'process models' that draw attention to different stages and activities in the translation of ideas into practical action. In schools, this is often tied into the natural rhythms of a school year.

As home–school matters come to be seen as matters of contractual obligation, rather than as voluntary extras, there will increasingly be a felt need to make statements of intent or to formulate policy or issue guidelines to colleagues. Current examples include the school brochure for new and prospective parents and

Record Sheet

Week ending _____ day, _____ 19__. School days in week _____

Set	Child's Name	Number of home reading sessions	Number absent	To be visited	COMMENTS Difficulties? Action needed
1.1	Alison Leach				
	Tracy Wharton				
	Sharon Young				
	Ian Boxley				
	Ricky Coles				
	Christopher Irving				
	William O'Sullivan				
	Scott Pinder				
	James Smith				
1.2	Jayne Barker				
	Juliette Grosvenor				
	Leanne White				
	Zahid Guizar				
	Kevin Hargreaves				
	Ajaib Hussein				
	Philip Nuttall				
	Martin Ratcliffe				
	Balal Shah				
	Andrew Taylor				
1.3	Patsy Carr				
	Andrea Dearden				
	Joanne Lock				
	Zia Abas				
	Martin Bell				
	Gary Holt				

Andy Boulter — infants teacher

"It has been an exciting experience to witness the removal of any 'them and us' barriers in such a way that links between home and school have grown together in a very positive way.

For the Belfield child, I think reading has been given its rightful place, becoming a natural family activity and not the imposed drudge which only takes place between 9.00 a.m. and 3.30 p.m. in a school building. Books have become a part of life and not an alien activity. It's good to know that our children enter the public library unafraid and willingly. So, probably, the most outstanding gain as I see it, is in terms of changing attitudes, and this includes teachers too."

One Week's Reading Card

John Bennett
(Child's name)   Week ending 4/6/1981

IN
_____ (Teacher) Belfield Community School

SUGGESTED READING

COMMENTS
Please initial if you hear your child read

WEEKEND		
Page 15, 16, 17	JB	good.
HOLIDAY EVENING		
Page 19.	JB	JOHN IS READING VERY WELL AT THIS MOMENT.
...ng	JB	STRUGGLED WITH COURSE AND COUNTED.
...ed il ...ING	JB	Good.
25		
...NING read up ...e 29	JB	good.

Beryl Page — former infants teacher

"I think we were all well aware, when the Project started, of the value of parental involvement in learning to read. It was our practice to send children's reading books home each day if parents were interested, (which many were), but not to insist when such interest seemed to be lacking. It was very noticeable that children who received such help seemed not only to do well with reading but also showed a more positive attitude to learning and to the life of school in general.

Our aim in the Project was to involve as many parents of our second years ('five pluses') as we could in daily ten minute reading sessions at home. By charting the results we hoped to prove in some way the immeasureable benefits to children of this kind of help.

Whatever statistics this exercise produces I for one a____ that the results are tremendously exciting. Every paren___ took up the challenge, some eagerly, some not really c___ they were capable of 'teaching'. One of the most hear___ that happened was that parents normally thought of t___ 'uninterested' or 'unco-operative' so far as education ___ were, in fact, deeply concerned with their child's pr___ those who did not have high hopes of their children's ___ ity were eventually persuaded, (or in a couple of cases ___ and for which I make no apologies) into realizing that t___ and their pleasure in, their involvement was extrem___ Parents began to notice facets of the learning proce___ children. For example, one parent said, "He reads ___ and doesn't know one word from another. He just looks at ___ and remembers the words". "Excellent", I said, "he's on the way", and went on to give helpful tips on the next step, for instance cover-ing up the picture and picking out an interesting noun.   Infant teachers know many 'tricks' to pass on to parents and this kind of interchange between parent and teacher can benefit children's ___

"We both hear Vicky read at night. First she learns the words from her older sister, then she reads it to the baby" said one parent. Another mother explained, "I read the pages to **Joanne** she reads them with me next, then tries them on her own. I talk about the pictures with her, asking about colours and what's happening. I sometimes ask her to find all the words like 'and' on the page and to pick out different words. She's played with books that she's made herself using the same words as those in her reading book. She draws the pictures and the teacher writes the words. At first Joanne was unhappy and didn't want to go to school because she was slow at her work. I don't think we're doing the teacher's job — we do something different and we can both work together".

One mother told us that she works in the evening but that **Natalie's** father and sister hear her read. "She's come on a lot more since she's been bringing her books home. I was surprised by her writing the other day. The windows were steamed up and Natalie wrote on them and spelt the words right too."

(Belfield Reading Project, 1981)

the staff handbook respectively. Such statements often make a very good set of reference points to which evaluation can be related.

Sometimes a more workable alternative to the examination of the whole programme is a focus upon a key event or form which seems likely to embody many of the wider issues and problems. In the present account, for example, teacher–parent interviews have been treated in this way – as a miniaturized version of home–school attitudes and practices as a whole.

ii) THE DEVELOPMENT OF APPROPRIATE MECHANISMS AND ACTIVITIES

Appoint a colleague to a post of responsibility for home–school matters. The job specification can make the task of initiating and co-ordinating evaluative activities explicit. (See p.18).

Fund a colleague (which may or may not be the above postholder) for a term's secondment within the present GRIST arrangements to monitor the institution's home–school programme. Use his or her report as the basis for staff discussion and policy making.

Set up a joint teacher–parent 'commission' with a brief to collect evidence rather than air exotic theories and unsupported prejudices. Use their findings as the basis of a joint review of existing arrangements.

Pair off colleagues (the 'third eye' approach) to monitor each other's work in this area.

Sponsor a number of small-scale activities, whose main task is to get a better picture of what parents think and feel and what their actual experience of dealing with their children's schools is like. This might include a survey, sample home visiting, surgeries and suggestion boxes, collecting questions at parents' evenings etc.

Enlist the help of students in initial training and on teaching practice to undertake studies of parental attitudes and experiences. It will help them and it will help you. It is also surprising what a bit of extra 'manpower' makes possible.

iii) THE DEVELOPMENT OF USEFUL METHODS AND TECHNIQUES

There is a steadily growing repertoire of available practical ideas, which draw upon the teacher-as-researcher and teacher–evaluator traditions. There is also plenty of scope for: the development of both imported and tailor-made methods and techniques, particularly those which build upon, and extend, the natural practice of teachers, their existing skill and knowledge; informal and more systematic approaches, reflecting both the school's normal ways of going about its work, the tackling of problems that arise and the need for periodic review; and individual and collaborative activity, within the school and directly involving parents and the wider community.

The organization of home–school thinking and practice

In this section the spotlight returns to the organization of home–school practice. Previously, however, the emphasis has been upon the planning, organization and evaluation of home–school arrangements as a whole. Here, by contrast, it is upon particular types of practice, together with a brief consideration of their respective strengths and weaknesses.

The section opens with a relatively detailed look at some of the complementary basic forms of home–school practice, which provide the foundations for a wider range of activity, as well as giving the programme much of its distinctive flavour. This is followed by a number of varied activities whose common link is their focus upon the curriculum and its relationships with a child's learning experience both in the classroom and in the home. Finally, the section closes with a brief look at a number of interesting current developments that are taking place, which reflect contemporary pressures and concerns, as well as a number of wider influences.

Getting down to basics: written communication and face-to-face contact

I have chosen to start looking at the basics with the examination of two widely-differing but equally familiar kinds of practical arrangement which, taken together, make up much of the 'bread and butter' of home–school communication and contact.

Written communication of one kind or another accounts for a great deal of the regular contact between a school and its parents. Although written materials can be produced in a variety of forms, to serve different purposes, I have chosen to give priority to brochures for new and prospective parents for reasons which will be made clear, and I have deliberately contrasted these with the problems of writing routine letters about a myriad of events and circumstances. This is completed by looking at face-to-face contact between parents and teachers, particularly that which stems from the arrangements that schools make for parents to discuss with their children's teachers, the progress children are making (usually called 'parents' evenings', 'consultations' or 'teacher–parent interviews').

These two contrasting examples have been chosen for a number of significant reasons. First, because they are virtually universal forms of practice. Since the 1980 Act, schools have been legally required to provide basic information for their parents. Teacher–parent interviews, however, have become established not by law but by 'custom and practice', although they are now rapidly acquiring the status of a contractual obligation. Secondly, both forms of contact are widely recognized as being (at least potentially) valuable and useful, by teachers and parents alike. In several recent studies of parental preferences, for example, both come out near the top of the list. In spite of this, the actual practice of schools in these areas leaves considerable room for improvement. Thirdly, written communication and face-to-face contact are, in many ways, complementary opposites, embodying widely differing, sometimes contradictory strengths and weaknesses. Each is very different yet, in its own ways, each is equally necessary. Put together, they raise most of the important problems of home–school communication, heightened because of the sharp contrasts they provide. Finally, because of their basic fundamental nature, the two forms make very good exemplars of home–school practice, raising many of the issues and organizational problems that are characteristic of the field as a whole and of attempts to bring about improvement within it.

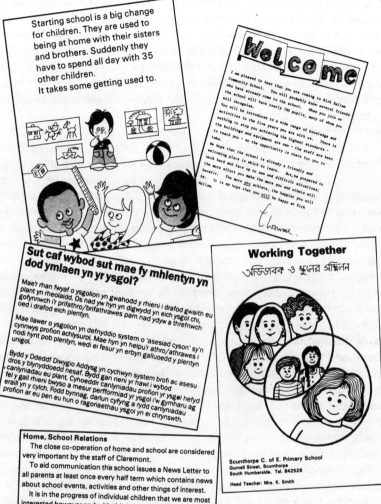

Starting school is a big change for children. They are used to being at home with their sisters and brothers. Suddenly they have to spend all day with 35 other children.
It takes some getting used to.

Welcome

I am pleased to hear that you are coming to Kirk Hallam Community School. You will probably know several friends who have already come to the school. When you join us the school will have nearly 700 pupils, many of whom you will recognise.
You will be introduced to a wide range of knowledge and activities in the five years you are with us. There is nothing to stop you achieving the highest standards – to teach you – so the opportunity is there for you to take.
We hope that the school is already a friendly and welcoming place in which to learn, but, be prepared to work hard and face up to new and difficult situations; the more effort you make the more you and others will benefit. The more *you* achieve, the happier you will be. It is my hope that you *will* be happy at Kirk Hallam.

Sut caf wybod sut mae fy mhlentyn yn dod ymlaen yn yr ysgol?

Mae'r rhan fwyaf o ysgolion yn gwahodd y rhieni i drafod gwaith eu plant yn rheolaidd. Os nad yw hyn yn digwydd yn eich ysgol chi, gofynnwch i'r prifathro/brifathrawes pam nad ydyw a threfnwch oed i drafod eich plentyn.

Mae llawer o ysgolion yn defnyddio system o 'asesiad cyson' sy'n cynnwys profion achlysurol. Mae hyn yn helpu'r athro/athrawes i nodi hynt pob plentyn, wedi ei fesur yn erbyn galluoedd y plentyn unigol.

Bydd y Ddeddf Diwygio Addysg yn cychwyn system brofi ac asesu dros y blynyddoedd nesaf. Bydd gan rieni yr hawl i wybod canlyniadau eu plant. Cyhoeddir canlyniadau profion yr ysgol hefyd fel y gall rhieni bwyso a mesur perfformiad yr ysgol i'w gymharu ag eraill yn y cylch. Fodd bynnag, darlun cyfyng a rydd canlyniadau profion ar eu pen eu hun o ragoriaethau ysgol yn ei chrynswth.

Home, School Relations

The close co-operation of home and school are considered very important by the staff of Claremont.

To aid communication the school issues a News Letter to all parents at least once every half term which contains news about school events, activities and other things of interest.

It is in the progress of individual children that we are most interested however and with this in mind a system of contact is used based upon reports and open evenings.

Working Together

অভিভাবক ও স্কুলের সম্মিলন

Scunthorpe C. of E. Primary School
Gurnell Street, Scunthorpe
South Humberside. Tel. 842526

Head Teacher: Mrs. K. Smith

Written communication

The written materials which schools produce, chiefly for their parents, are an important but often neglected feature of their contact with the outside world. Within a diversity of form and content, such materials – whether consciously or not – carry important messages about a school's intentions and practices, project images of its life and work and help to define the relationship which it seeks with parents and the wider community. It is also clear that the appraisal of their efforts in this area is a task that schools can and should undertake, which has considerable benefit and value.

In the first place, such an examination inevitably raises wider and deeper issues. It is, for example, almost impossible to make judgements about materials, without asking questions about the purposes they are meant to fulfil, the situations they are designed to meet, and the audiences for whom they are intended. Similarly, descriptions of arrangements that exist and of provision that is made, sooner or later require some evaluation of their effectiveness. The pattern where a school, attempting to improve and develop particular practices, is obliged to consider and respond to wider and deeper issues, is now a familiar feature of professional development and school reform. So the task of reviewing its written communications is a task well-suited to a school's INSET arrangements and can often serve as a catalyst for developing the skills of collaborative working as much as for bringing about progress and change in the home–school area itself.

Written communication represents one form of tangible evidence about what a school believes and does. At worst, it may be little more than glossy, rather empty, window-dressing. My experience, on the other hand, has been that it provides an important opportunity to re-appraise what a school has to offer and to relate this, in appropriate ways, to the lives and experience of parents and the wider community. For the task of extending and improving the quality of a school's written communications is one where, with some effort and imagination, considerable and even dramatic improvements can be made. Unlike many suggestions for educational innovation and change, such a task does not call for complicated organizational changes, or additional staffing and resources. More than anything else it calls for the harnessing of the goodwill and honest intentions which I believe the vast majority of teachers still have towards their parents and the wider community, in spite of the setbacks of recent years.

During the course of a typical year, schools produce a variety of written materials, often on a prodigious scale. This will incorporate the following.

- The requirements of the 1980 Education Act – a very minimal set of requirements for basic information associated with the parental choice of schools and the publication of exam results. The 1988 Act follows this by requiring schools to make test results available to the parents of individual pupils. This is an even more contentious area with far reaching implications for home–school relations.
- The dictates of LEA policies in a number of different areas, e.g. curriculum policies, home–school relations, equal opportunities policies, etc.
- The requirements of the particular type of school or phase of schooling, e.g. starting school, choosing subject options, etc.

- The still extensive scope that individual schools have to decide what they will communicate about to parents, and when and how this will be done.

In choosing to illustrate this range and variety, I have chosen to examine two well-established, universal forms of written communication which serve very different purposes in widely differing ways and which serve as complementary opposites in illustrating their respective strengths and weaknesses.

School brochures are important because they represent, first, an obligation, backed by law, to inform new and prospective parents about the way the school operates (complemented by the 1986 Act, which offers a similar opportunity to established parents, via the annual report). Secondly, an opportunity for schools to provide a considered, extended statement about what it is trying to do together with an account of how it attempts to do this; and thirdly, one of the first contacts for new parents with their children's school. As we all know, first impressions are very important. Additionally, many parents have indicated that they continue to use school brochures as a source of reference, particularly when they want to check out organizational matters or particular policies, when issues and problems arise at a later stage. Alternatively, letters and newsletters are produced with relentless regularity, as a function of the complexity of a school's business and the broad nature of its responsibilities; and constitute the basic bread and butter of written communication, often produced in a great hurry, as the cheapest and quickest way of sending out information on a large scale. This does not, of course, apply to personal, handwritten letters sent out by headteachers, pastoral staff and form tutors or classteachers. Because of the circumstances in which letters home are produced, a school's guard can slip, to reveal its true attitudes towards parents!

EXAMINING SCHOOL PROSPECTUSES AND BROCHURES

In an earlier, collaborative report I developed a framework, based on the examination of hundreds of real-life examples, for comparing brochures, for analysing some of their obvious features and, above all, for identifying the kinds of purpose they are attempting to serve. Indeed, judging from the feedback that I still get, it appears not only to have stood the test of time, but in addition, draws attention to some of the special problems engendered by a combination of contemporary circumstances – competition between schools with falling rolls, declining budgets and the relentless approach to a consumerist approach to schooling by a single-minded government.

The following framework identifies four distinct, though sometimes overlapping, sets of intentions and purposes:
- the provision of basic information;
- improving the public image;
- tackling developmental concerns; and,
- encouraging parental involvement

The four stranded framework for analysing school prospectuses and brochures gives particular emphasis to their content and organization and, especially, to the impact of the brochure as a whole. Equally important, however, is the skill of developing a critical feel for the texture of the language, which is

The provision of basic information
- Main purpose is to transmit basic factual information to parents (in line with recent Education Acts, LEA format etc.).
- Emphasizes organizational efficiency rather than educational processes.
- Regards information giving as straightforward and unproblematic.
- Implies a rather limited role for parents, in terms of their unconditional support for the school, on *its* terms.
- Usually embodies traditional values and practices.

Typical features
- Detailed information about what is required for the smooth and orderly running of the school.
- Considerable emphasis upon school rules and pupil behaviour, uniform, homework, etc.

Improving the public image
- Projects an *image* of the school which is based upon the careful selection and organization of content, in a style which is thought to invite acceptance and approval.
- Tailors the brochure as a response to the established needs, aspirations and anxieties of identified groups or types of parent. A potent, contemporary version of this approach is currently displayed by the school which responds to anxieties about falling rolls by attempting to move 'upmarket', to recruit more 'desirable' or influential parents or to improve a poor or negative reputation.

Typical features
- Emphasis upon the 'vote-winning' aspects of education, such as levels of formal academic achievement, firm discipline.
- Emphasis upon traditional standards and forms such as the teaching of Latin, emphasis upon 'the basics', provision of out of school activities such as school clubs and trips abroad, the formal qualifications of staff etc.

Tackling developmental concerns

This approach focuses attention upon key moments in the school careers of pupils by concerning itself with important features of context and circumstance:

- starting school, transition from infant to junior, transfer from primary to secondary school
- the move from relatively small to much larger and more complex units of organization (e.g. small rural primary schools)
- the practical problems created by parental choice, where these are reinforced by LEA policies, which can necessitate a number of visits to (secondary) schools, before parental preferences are declared.

The developmental needs of schools, families and, especially, pupils at the different stages of their education

Typical features

Special emphasis upon entry or transfer arrangements. Constructive suggestions for easing transition for both parents and pupils.

Encouraging parental involvement

- Brochure seen as only a small part of a developing programme of opportunities for contact and involvement. Written communication is no substitute for personal contact.
- Implies a fuller role for parents, within an educational partnership as educators themselves, within the home setting, and as active supporters of their children's work at school.
- Emphasis upon educational processes in general and the quality of pupil learning in particular.

Typical features

- Emphatic welcome to new parents and stress upon the opportunities to develop positive relationships.
- Details of arrangements for further contact and involvement.
- Suggestions about 'How parents can help their children learn'. (See pages 60–63)

crucially determined by its tone and style. There is, for example, a particular kind of 'teacher language', that I have worked hard, but obviously unsuccessfully, to avoid in my own life, since my children recognize it a mile off. 'Talking like a teacher' is most off-putting to those outside of schools.

'How parents can help...' both at school and in the home would, on the face of it, seem to be a crucially important area for schools to think through, preferably in partnership with the parents of the children they teach. In fact it is not a topic for which schools are legally required to provide information; neither is it, in practice, an issue which many schools have chosen to tackle in their brochures and prospectuses, although the number that do so is steadily growing. What is clear, however, as the following examples show all too clearly, is that when schools do tackle this issue, in whatever style and form they choose, the results are deeply revealing of their fundamental attitudes, not only to parents as educators, but to home–school relations in general. Because of this, it makes an excellent example for the close and detailed study of written communication, both in one's own work and in that of other people.

SOME COMMON CRITICISMS OF SCHOOL BROCHURES

In the preceding section, I have been concerned to develop a classification of brochures, as a way of bringing out their special, distinctive features and characteristics. This section by contrast, sketches in a number of criticisms that seem to apply to a large majority of materials that we have examined at Nottingham. Many of them apply equally to other forms of written communication to parents.

First, many brochures suffer from a confusion of purpose and a lack of clear intentions. They often attempt to serve a number of different functions but do not distinguish sharply enough between them or attempt to tackle them separately. Such a lack of explicit aims often means, in practice, that the messages in one section cancel out or neutralize those in another. A genuinely warm welcome, for example, can easily be swamped if followed by exhaustive information about school rules or procedures for visiting. Similarly, the task of conveying images of the school as a whole can be difficult to reconcile with the need for clear and concise information on specific topics. In the end the brochure or pamphlet fails to achieve a clear identity and seems muddled, confused and self-cancelling.

Almost all the brochures that we have seen seem weak on context, in one or more of the following areas:

i) The context of entry to the school, and the need to build relationships with new sets of pupils and parents.

ii) The context of the home–school programme as a whole, and those other occasions for contact and the sharing of ideas, experience and problems.

iii) The social context of the school, and the interests attitudes, values and experience of parents as a whole, and variations between them.

Many brochures, indeed, appear so lacking in context that they seem, for all intents and purposes, to have been designed in a vacuum or by a computer programme. The extent of this criticism is sometimes brought home by the exceptions, such as brochures produced in other languages for communities whose mother tongue is not English, or the occasional reference to parental anxieties which reveals some imaginative empathy for the parents' eye view of the world.

The content and tone of too much of this material still seems to be prescriptive and negative. 'Thou shalt not...' is a teacher imperative that seems to be dying slowly and painfully. Statements of school rules, whether whole or paraphrased, are a good example of such a criticism, in both a literal and a symbolic form. They are almost always concerned with what you *can't* do, with what is forbidden or, at least, discouraged. An interesting and highly specific illustration of negative attitudes occurs in the frequent advice about television viewing habits for parents of new intakes of primary school children. Here the focus is almost always on the (unproven) dangers to the mind and body of extended and undiscriminating watching, rather than to the undoubted educational gains of selective viewing. In terms of communication and meanings they are not the same message!

A very common feature of many brochures, and one which reveals a number of basic omissions of design and planning, is that they are too verbose and too verbal. We have seen many examples of materials which occupy an extensive acreage of close print. In some cases, we have been hard-pressed to imagine any parents having the stamina or the application to hack their way through the dense jungle of verbiage.

Another aspect of brochure verbosity is the implicit, but nevertheless real reliance upon the written word as the ultimate form of communication. The weakness of this exaggerated faith in the written word has been brought home to us by those schools who have occasionally attempted to convey information and messages diagrammatically, or in other visual forms such as cartoons, or through the imaginative layout of carefully selected contents on a page, using different sizes of type or double columns.

Such criticisms draw attention to the lack of selection in much brochure design. First, there is the lack of selection concerning contents. It seems to us, for example, difficult to justify enormously extended whole staff lists, particularly for large comprehensive schools. Similarly, we cannot see how parents can handle very complicated maps of the whole school site or elaborate information about the arrangements for medical inspections.

The second aspect of selection focus highlights the criticism that schools do not present information economically. It seems to me a curious irony that many teachers in the classroom spend time trying to persuade their pupils that economy of expression and clarity of thought go hand in glove!

Finally, we have been surprised to discover how little attention most brochures pay to the process of education itself, which is, self-evidently, one of the central reasons for the existence of schools in our society. Introductory brochures may not be the only, or the best, place to introduce a discussion of teaching methods or other curricular issues. However, the total omission, in many cases, of *any* reference to them, seems to us bound to convey the message that the school considers such matters to be beyond the legitimate interest or concern of parents.

HOW CAN YOU HELP
AS A PARENT ?

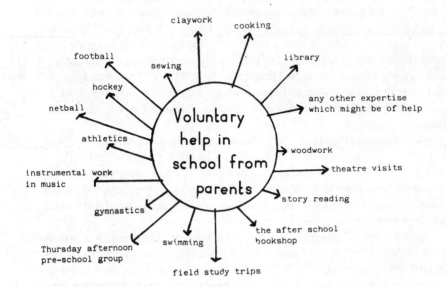

Voluntary help in school from parents

- claywork
- cooking
- library
- any other expertise which might be of help
- woodwork
- theatre visits
- story reading
- the after school bookshop
- field study trips
- swimming
- Thursday afternoon pre-school group
- gymnastics
- instrumental work in music
- athletics
- netball
- hockey
- football
- sewing

How can you help your child before he/she starts school ?

Can he tie his own shoelaces?

Can she button her coat ?

You can help your child most by teaching him/her to do ordinary things which save time for the teacher. If your child can dress themselves, fasten their own shoes, button their coats or zip their anoraks we would be very grateful.

You can help us by reading stories to your child so that they are interested in books and learn new words.

If they want to write their name, then please teach

How can you help
at school ?

The main way to help the school is to let your child see that you take an interest in what he or she does at school and that you are keen for him or her to achieve the best. Praise progress and build up the self-confidence of your child in his or her own ability and encourage him or her to join in all that Alumwell offers. There are many lunchtime and after school clubs and societies which will help your child to develop friendships and interests.

When necessary do all in your power to lead your child to respect the school and follow its rules so helping us to maintain a pleasant school atmosphere.

Please make the effort to come and see us at open evenings and to attend school functions.

LISTEN as well as talk to him. If possible sit down by your child when he is talking to you so that he isn't hustled by the feeling that you are going to dash off without warning. We often deny a child the chance to talk to us because we are in a hurry. May be we cut him short with "I'll be with you in a minute, dear" - but if we do come back in a minute he may have forgotten what he wanted to say. Try to show that words are important because they are ways of conveying feelings to other people, thus enabling them to understand our needs.

HELP him to recognise his own printed name using the small script letters he will use when he comes to write in school.

Encourage your child to ask questions and always take time to answer or show him or her where to look for the answer.

Take your child on visits to places of local interest and talk together about what you have seen.

Help your child to value homework. This is a unique opportunity for your son or daughter to develop a regular habit of learning and to study independently We ask every pupil to do regular homework and we give your child a Homework Note-book. Your interest and sharing with this activity can further our joint responsibility for the development of your child. (During the first year we would not expect the homework to take more than one hour each school night).

We invite you to sign the homework diaries each week and please use it to let us know of any ideas or problems you or your child have experienced.

abcdefghijk
lmnopqrstuv
wxyz.

TO HELP YOUR CHILD

When your child starts school for the very first time, it may be a sad occasion for you, it may be joyful, it may even be difficult. Whichever is the case, the following points will be of help to you, your child and the staff. Please read them carefully and see if you can help by:

1 MARKING ALL YOUR CHILD'S CLOTHING CLEARLY WITH THE NAME.

2 Leaving your child at the School Gate after the first two or three days. If you are meeting him/her out of school, please wait outside the gate and do not go to the classrooms as the staff will be very busy making sure that all coats, etc. are with the proper owners!

3 Giving your child the correct dinner money (day;   week).

4 Giving any private information about your child on enrolment. This may include details about asthma, eyesight, hearing, etc.

5 SEEING ME, AND NOT THE STAFF, WITH ANY PROBLEMS. UNDER NO CIRCUMSTANCES SHOULD PARENTS MAKE THEIR WAY TO THE CLASSROOMS WITHOUT FIRST OBTAINING THE APPROVAL OF THE HEADMASTER, OR, IN HIS ABSENCE, THE DEPUTY-HEAD, THE SCHOOL SECRETARY OR WELFARE ASSISTANT.

6 Teaching your child before he/she comes to school to tie and untie shoes laces and ties, to go to the toilet properly, to use a knife and fork correctly, to dress and undress, to wash and dry hands. These are most useful and save a great deal of a teacher's time.

7 Allowing your child a SMALL amount of pocket money each week for sweets and crisps at the School Shop. If you can afford this, and agree with the practice, it is excellent training.

8 Making sure your child knows WHERE to GET ON/OFF the special bus if he/she is to travel on it.

9 Teaching kerb drill a little time on this could save life.

10 MAKING SURE THAT YOUR CHILD KNOWS WHERE HE/SHE LIVES AND ALSO A TELEPHONE NUMBER (if applicable) FOR CONTACTING YOU IN AN EMERGENCY.

HELPING AT SCHOOL

1 *Reading Help* Some parents are already helping with reading sessions and are proving very helpful. Though not actually teaching reading, such things as listening to children read, checking their 'long word jig-saws' or 'snake games' or being a 'word-bingo caller' for a small group is very valuable (The first session is spent in explaining to parents exactly what to do). If anyone is free to help, please let me know.

2 Talking about an interesting hobby e.g. stamp collecting, model making, rock finding, pigeons, especially if you have na interesting collection or slides.

3 Accompanying a class on a visit or Youth hostelling week- end (sorry! no young children can be brought).

4 Working with children or staff to make things for school e.g. painting, sewing, woodwork, music, drama, modelling.

5 Helping to run an after school club 4.00 p.m.   5.00 p.m.

6 Helping with refreshments at a disco or parents function.

7 Have you any contact in social life or at work where you can get items (free or very cheap) which would be useful in school e.g. waste material of any sort for collage work, off-cuts of wood, card or other material?

8 Is there anything you can make well (e.g. soft toys, leather goods) which we would be able to sell at school reasonably priced, but at a profit, the school paying for the materials?

9 Have you any other special talents to offer which we may be able to use e.g. 'make-up', or making scenery, or costumes for school play or Christmas performance?

Apart from these, the main way to help the school is to let your children see that you take an interest in what they do at school and that you are keen for them to do their best. Don't forget to ask them about what they have done and give time to listen to them.

Please make the effort to come up and see the teacher at open evenings and to attend school functions, especially if you are invited to see your child doing something at school.

Ways in which you can help

Early bedtimes for your child, including Sunday.
Spend *time* with your child not just money on him.
Take an interest in school affairs.
Read to your child and hear him read.
Library membership is an excellent thing.
Encourage punctuality, good attendance, good manners towards other children and adults.
Trust school decisions.
Make every effort to allow your child to go on class outings, then he can participate in follow-up work.
Encourage loyalty to school group activities games teams, concert performances.
Do not hesitate to come to school to talk over problems.
We hope that this sort of homeschool association will produce happy children who are socially well adjusted and proud of their growing achievements.
We confidently count on your co-operation.

How parents help the School

The following are some of the ways in which you, our parents, can help us in school:
by:-
checking and unpacking stock
making simple booklets
duplicating worksheets
accompanying a teacher on a local visit with children
carrying out simple repairs to books and equipment
hearing children read
helping with needlecraft and cookery
assisting with football/netball
offering time and transport for longer trips
making curtains, aprons and costumes
making tea for meetings
playing the piano for choir, class music
being on a rota of swimming observers
helping at the swimming baths
collecting bank money
running the School Bookshop
stamping school books
covering books
providing simple carft resources wood, material
collecting waste paper
offering a talent you have dancing, flower arranging.

Parents and School

In a school such as this I do not think it is necessary to have a *formal* Parent Teacher Association. What is, however, absolutely vital is mutual understanding and co- operation between Home and School, and I do hope that we can rely upon your *help* and *involvement* in our activities. We can't draw a firm dividing line between what your child learns at home and what he learns in school. Parents and teachers are *partners* and in our particular case we have an excellent opportunity to demonstrate what can be achieved when we work happily together. Here are some suggestions for future activities involving parents.

1 Making and mending apparatus and toys.
2 Making costumes for plays.
3 Arranging flowers.
4 Assisting with preparation of craft materials.
5 Fathers doing 'odd jobs' making display stands.
6 Helping at school functions sports days, concerts etc.
7 Helping teacher on out-of-school visits and excursions.
8 Helping with cookery.
9 Helping at Christmas parties.
10 Raising money for School Funds.

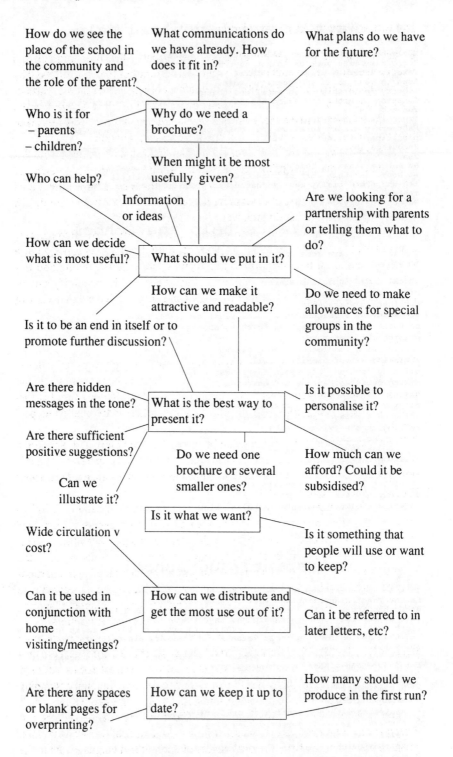

How do we see the place of the school in the community and the role of the parent?

What communications do we have already. How does it fit in?

What plans do we have for the future?

Who is it for
– parents
– children?

Why do we need a brochure?

When might it be most usefully given?

Who can help?

Information or ideas

Are we looking for a partnership with parents or telling them what to do?

How can we decide what is most useful?

What should we put in it?

How can we make it attractive and readable?

Do we need to make allowances for special groups in the community?

Is it to be an end in itself or to promote further discussion?

Are there hidden messages in the tone?

What is the best way to present it?

Is it possible to personalise it?

Are there sufficient positive suggestions?

Can we illustrate it?

Do we need one brochure or several smaller ones?

How much can we afford? Could it be subsidised?

Is it what we want?

Wide circulation v cost?

Is it something that people will use or want to keep?

Can it be used in conjunction with home visiting/meetings?

How can we distribute and get the most use out of it?

Can it be referred to in later letters, etc?

How many should we produce in the first run?

Are there any spaces or blank pages for overprinting?

How can we keep it up to date?

Figure 3.5: Brochures – some key questions (From: Bastiani, J. (ed) *Written Communication Between Home and School*. University of Nottingham School of Education)

EXAMINING LETTERS AND NEWSLETTERS

Letters to parents, on a variety of topics, are probably the most frequent and widely-used form of contact between schools and families (closely followed by the' phone, judged by my own efforts to contact colleagues in schools, particularly before 9.30am!). Whilst the content and form of most of these would seem to be too ordinary to make them worth a second glance, it is precisely this taken for grantedness that makes them worthy of closer examination.

The cumulative impact of a succession of letters, often in a similar vein, reveals, and systematically reinforces a school's attitudes towards its parents and its perceptions of their value in their children's schooling. I have often heard parents say in the context of describing the arrival of a letter from school, 'Oh no, not again!', or, 'What do they want *this* time?'.

In attempting to understand such reactions, it is a useful, and often salutary experience, to examine the output of your school's letters, over a period of a year, in relation to: recurring topics and themes (obsessions); timing and frequency; and content, style and tone. From this, it is possible to identify a number of areas and ways in which improvement and constructive alternatives can be identified.

Practical suggestions

Most letters are often extremely blunt and impersonal in their forms of address. For example, 'Dear Parents' is often a very crude way of beginning, given the complexities of many family set-ups. In many cases it is relatively simple to arrange for teachers or pupils themselves, to address letters individually and personally.

In my experience letters could often be more effectively targeted. Sending a blanket letter to all parents, that concerns the activities and experience of a minority seems a blunt instrument and, in some cases – for instance moans about truancy – can be rightly resented.

School letters nearly always seem to have a particular look and feel, recognizable at a great distance. Information about particular events or activities might be more effectively conveyed in the form of a small handbill, or reinforced by a mention in other places, e.g. newsletter or posters displayed in the neighbourhood. Above all, schools probably produce too many letters, particularly of a routine kind, and should concentrate on reducing their sheer volume and frequency. This can sometimes be done by better planning and by combining messages, perhaps in more accessible forms like newsletters.

Like other forms of home–school communication, letters to parents are more likely to be effective when they are part of a broad and varied home–school programme, with plenty of opportunities to get to know the school and its teachers, to find out the things that they want to know and to develop their understanding of what is going on, both in the classroom and in the school as a whole.

I do not believe that there is any mystique about writing effective letters, just a need for a certain amount of imagination and a great deal of care. Attention needs to be paid not only to obvious matters of content and language, but to the wider issues of context and audience, as well as to neglected features like layout and design. Perhaps it is helpful to think of letter writing against a checklist of positive qualities. I believe that, as far as possible, letters should be:

Clear
Direct
Economical
Honest
Informal
Friendly
Personal
Reassuring

But perhaps these qualities should be a feature of *all* effective communication with parents – written or otherwise!

There is a danger in this account of treating newsletters only as a way of easing the pressure on the over-production of routine letters containing basic information about school arrangements, events and activities. This would, however, be enormously unfortunate in the way it underestimates the rich potential of school (and class) newsletters, although it is a potential that is a yet largely unrealized. For newsletters have the capability of acting as a vehicle for very different kinds and forms of communication, in which a number of different things can happily co-exist, such as:

- the personal account, based on recent experience with the more general consideration of broad educational issues;
- the lighthearted and the serious;
- from information-giving to the beginning of a process of consultation about particular issues or policies.

In short, the newsletter is a polyglot form that thrives on diversity of content and style. It can also embody a compromise between relatively cheap, quick and easy production and something that is more solid, durable and reflective. Above all, however, a newsletter is an ideal medium for the combined effort of teachers, parents and pupils in:

- recognizing and representing their different perspectives and experience, (as well as their common ground);
- incorporating joint planning, production and distribution, thus pooling ideas and sharing the effort; and,
- providing a platform for a broad editorial front and a wide range of contributions.

'IT AINT WHAT YOU DO, IT'S THE WAY THAT YOU DO IT'

We live – as we're constantly being reminded – in an electronic age, in which our thinking and feeling are powerfully shaped by media images in advertising and magazines, video and television. Has *your* school come out of the Gutenberg era yet? My impression is that dense acres of barely readable, boring verbiage, printed on medieval equipment, is going to find it difficult to compete in a post-industrial, hi-tech, tabloid world. But let's not get too suicidal about this! There *are* signs of both survival and partial recovery. Though progress in this area is patchy, there seems to be a more 'professional' approach to matters of design and layout, with greater attention given to organization and format, language and the quality of reproduction. Particular examples would include the design of multiform materials for pupils and their parents, written materials in different mother tongues, the development of dynamic school newsletters and the use of handbills to replace certain kinds of basic letter.

Face to face contact

There are, or should be, many wide-ranging opportunities for face to face contact between teachers and parents. These can range from classroom and curriculum-related activities to social and fundraising events and from one-to-one encounters to work with small groups, with parents of year groups or, from time to time, with the parent body as a whole.

In this section I have chosen to concentrate upon teacher – parent interviews (or 'parents evenings' as they are rather misleadingly called) as representative of this range of possibilities. I have done this in the confident knowledge that many other forms of face to face contact are examined elsewhere in the book (e.g. curriculum evenings, working in classrooms, annual meetings under the aegis of the 1986 Act, home visiting etc.) Mainly, however, I have done so because the arrangements that schools make for teachers and parents to meet, to review on a regular semi-formal basis the progress of individual pupils, contain a paradox that lies at the heart of much – school activity.

The problem to be resolved is this; while both teachers and parents continue to strongly support the *idea* of the usefulness of such contacts, there is clear evidence that both find the actual *experience* of such events disappointing, unproductive, and often deeply frustrating. There is clearly a wide gulf between the high hopes and good intentions of teachers and parents and what actually takes place in the name of consultation, in thousands of schools several times a year.

One of the problems that I have encountered on many occasions in working with teachers to resolve this paradox and find practical ways forward, is the very problem of routine familiarity that such meetings embody. The whole business is enmeshed in a jungle of deeply ingrained assumptions and practices. What is needed, at the outset, is ways of breaking this pattern – of looking at teacher–parent interviews from a different angle or through fresh eyes.

Some of the devices that we have found useful for doing this include:
- Tape recording yourself at the next parents' evening and examining what takes place (behind locked doors!).
- Planning to analyse your next consultation event using the enclosed framework and questions (p.75)
- Collecting different kinds of 'evidence' of what goes on at one of your parents evenings, e.g. questionnaire surveys, interviews, making a video.
- Using a 'third eye' approach, pairing up with a colleague and looking at each other's work in this area.
- Visiting another school's parents' evening, by arrangement.
- Drawing, where appropriate, upon your own experience of your own children's arrangements to discuss their progress with their teachers.

'All the children's books would be out and the place would be milling with parents and there was no sort of, erm, privacy. The teacher sort of looked around and thought, 'Are you next? Or you?! and you'd sit around saying 'After you' and getting more and more furious. And if you had three children, you were there most of the night! . . . By the time you got to your third teacher, at nine thirty, you were worn to a frazzle . . ' (Parent)

* * * * * * * *

'I do occasionally see the teacher, but only if I've got a problem, I don't like to be running up to the school every five minutes sort of thing. Because, well, the teachers do know roughly what they're doing, don't they?' (Parent)

* * * * * * * *

'Personally, I don't think that a school presenting itself to you gives you that true a picture. I think the way to find out about a school is to go down and see and then maybe look around the school and talk to the teacher, your child's teacher' (Parent)

* * * * * * * *

'The prime objective of parents evenings is to discuss the work. What he needs at home, if anything; what he needs at school, if anything, that's different from what is happening now.' (Parent)

You get to know some things that really help. I had one boy, he was fascinated by birds and really knowledgeable about them – I never knew that until his mum told me at a parents' evening.' (Teacher)

* * * * * * * *

'It's lip-service really, isn't it? You can't get anything meaningful said in that short time, but I suppose you have to do it. It's really accountability isn't it?' (Teacher)

The following illustration, which is a ten year old's view of such an occasion, is also *most* revealing:

Underlying most of these suggestions, however, is the need to anchor any discussion that takes place in the critical examination of real examples and actual situations. To illustrate something of this process, two examples are now given, followed by a brief analysis which draws out a number of considerations of practical value.

- What is going on here?
- What do the 'ground rules' seem to be?
- Are the different parties in this encounter 'on the same wavelength'?
- Do these exchanges seem familiar to you as a teacher or parent or both?

The first thing that has to be said is that there are extracts from a *real* parents' evening. The infant school in which it is set claims that it has 'good' relationships with its parents and that this is one of a number of formal and informal opportunities for teachers and parents to meet.

Secondly, I have used these particular interviews, and others like it, as a way of opening-up discussion with groups of teachers and parents in many parts of Britain, where I have been rather taken aback by the similarity of response that I have encountered. Teachers say that it is typical of many such teacher–parent interviews. Parents say that they have experienced such encounters many times (as do teachers talking about visiting their own children's schools)! Primary and secondary teachers also add that, in essence, it is the kind of encounter that is characteristic of their kinds of school too.

Table 3.2: Teacher–parent interview 1*

Teacher	Well, he's working quite hard. I'm quite pleased with his work.
Mother	Mm.
Teacher	He's quite good at maths. This is the maths book he's done at the moment, er, it's, in fact it's just addition, but I – we do it in a lot of different ways [yeah] so that hopefully when ever they're faced with any type of problem, well, they just cope with it.
Mother	Yeah. Yeah.
Teacher	And all this, which is just counting; count backwards, count forwards, count sideways.
Mother	I noticed that he was good at maths.
Teacher	Yes. Yes.
Mother	I'm glad about that [he is] 'cos I was never good at . . .
Teacher	Yes, he is good, [Yeah. Yeah] but he grasps it very quickly [Yeah] and easily, so that's quite nice [*pause*]. These are, um, television books, that's a book – 'cos we do watch a television programme, and then they have to write about it, of course. [Oh, I see, yeah] so, er, this is his current book. His writing writing is a bit untidy [Mm] as you can see [Yeah] but er, there's a lot of it.
Mother	I've said that to Mrs. T. the last time [Yes] I said I wasn't very pleased with it [Yes] but she says . . .
Teacher	Yes, well it's improving, you see, I [she thought it was all right, yeah] like a nicely presented page [I do, I think it's nice to see that they're . . .] but if it means that they only write a little of nice writing, I'd rather have a lot of untidy writing, if it's good [yeah] interesting stuff [yeah]. Some of them write a lot and it's, it's repetition and [yeah] so on, but *his* work's quite nice, he works quite hard. He does tend to natter, you know, [Yeah] he'll talk with anybody who happens to sit next to him. [Yeah] He *does* sometimes waste a bit of time but, he's very good really, in that if you say 'Now look, S., come *on* [Yeah] you've got a lot to do today', then he does, [he does it, yeah] he gets on and does it. He works hard [yeah]. He's got a good attitude to work. You know, each page, he doesn't skimp, he does exactly the amount [yeah] of which I . . . he *knows* I expect, and sometimes if he gets really interested, he'll do two pages, so [yeah] I'm quite pleased with his attitude to work

* It is a pity that space doesn't allow for the quotation of complete transcripts. For within the framework of the interview as a whole, including the way it is launched and brought to a close, important general issues are raised and relationships more fully revealed.

Table 3.3: Teacher–parent interview 2

Teacher	I'm really pleased, I mean, every day it's a bit better. This is yesterday. And I, I can see the improvement there.
Mother	[*Very quietly*] But he's not very good at reading, is he?
Teacher	Well [*pause*] let me have a look, which book is he on? [Erm] They've not got their books home tonight ['Something and the...' I think] I've kept them in the drawer at the moment. Ah! now he's just changed on to the new erm...
Mother	[*Loudly, over the top of teacher*] He's just changed opticians you see. She said his eyes were no better, like [yes] and she says until he focuses right, I think he goes again next month [yes] 'cos they didn't know whether to send him to the hospital you see. [Yes] She said forget about it, but you can't.
Teacher	No, you can't. No, I can understand that. Now, I've put him as it were, back. [Yeah] You probably realized [yeah] the – it's an easier book, but I've done this with about ten of the children because I wanted them to try this new reading scheme we've got, and I'm doing a topic on it at the moment. [yes] We're doing a lot of work on it, and so he's gone back, because he's got to learn the names of the people [yeah] in the stories. And he's reading them quite nicely. He's reading them quite quickly. So, I think he'd sooner get up to his own level [yeah] but, he was stuck on those other books, and there's no point in pushing a reading scheme or [No] a book [that's when he came home] if he's bored [yeah] and he *was*, and I was too! [Yeah] [*joint laughter*] So, ... 'cos he'd been on it so long, you know, and it was getting awful and depressing [yeah] for him. And these are nice stories, they're thin little books, short stories, and he's getting through them, [yeah] so that's why it appears he's gone back – he's not really, it's just that, if they ever change reading schemes, they've got to go down a bit, otherwise [yeah] there's just a lot of names and places, and they don't know what they are. *That's* depressing. Has he brought those home?
Mother	That one, yeah.
Teacher	Yes, [I've listened to that] I've not heard him today, so he'll read this to me tomorrow presumably and [yeah] then change it, and you see they're so short that they can change it in a day. [Mm] read it in once [yeah] and they can get a new book, and that's good for them, so, we'll see how he gets on. I must admit, I was a bit concerned about it, 'cos it, [yeah] wasn't on a level with his maths, and the way that he's been writing, but, if it *is* his eyes, then it's quite possible that he just simply can't focus [Yeah, yeah, that's what *she* said] to that extent, [yeah] so we'll just plod on slowly, 'cos to rush him and put him off reading would be fatal, [yeah] 'cos he, you know, he's, he's, bright enough.
Mother	I'm glad he's behaving a bit more though. [*joint laughter*] It worried me to death.

For some time I have felt, here as elsewhere in the development of more effective home–school relations, that a good place to start is with a critical look
at existing arrangements. So let us return to our two examples. It seems clear to
me that the teacher and the parents have different 'agendas'. Each has a different, and rather incompatible, notion of the purpose of the meeting. The teacher
appears to be giving a 'verbal report', and so would see the parents' attempts to
engage her in discussion as interruptions.

In the second extract in particular, the mother sees the occasion, (especially
in the interview as a whole) as the appropriate occasion for exploring some of
the problems concerning her son's welfare and progress, about which she is deeply troubled. As a result of this mis-match of purposes she is continuously over-
ruled and put down. It is equally obvious that one of the parties does much more
talking than the other. Moreover, 'teacher talk' has a rather distinctive quality,
redolent of encounters with other authority figures and very unlike the conver-
sational lives of most parents. Little wonder, then, that many parents that I have
listened to in the course of my work (and I, as a parent myself) dismiss a great
deal of teacher talk as 'flannel' or 'bull' and describe teachers as 'word mer-
chants'. Such a reaction can also be seen in the context of the general absence
of systematic or organized evidence about their child's general performance or
particular problems. I am particularly reminded of this by some of my more recent work, which stresses the variety of evidence that parents look for in making, and sustaining, judgements about their children's progress (see Chapter 3).

Finally, there is a curious quality about this and other teacher–parent interviews which becomes more apparent and tension-ridden as children get older
and more independent. It stems from the reality in which (like the Les Dawson
joke) two interested parties are discussing a third in his or her absence. This
often serves to give a spurious or collusive quality to the proceedings. It certainly limits both the picture that emerges and the possibilities for constructive
action.

THE TEACHER'S VIEWPOINT ABOUT PARENTS' EVENINGS

Comments like those shown below echo around the staffroom as the event re-
morselessly comes round again. Record books are brought up-to-date, the classroom is made more attractive, the children's books are gathered in for inspection
as teachers prepare for that face to face encounter with the people most intimate-
ly involved with the children they teach – the parents.

> You never get the parents you want to see.
> They're not really necessary. I see most of my parents when they bring the
> kids to school and they can chat if they want to.
> They're a bit of an ordeal, really – I mean, 25 parents to get through in one
> evening.
> I suppose they're useful. When you see some parents, you understand the
> problems their kids have.
> Exhausting – but necessary.

Teachers vary in what they feel about such a meeting and also in what they see
as the purposes of it. Some emphasize the part it plays in establishing and main-
taining good personal relationships with parents; others see it as an opportunity
to get parental backing for the school's teaching methods; some wish to ensure

that parents are aware of children's behavioural difficulties; there are those who use it to learn more about the children, particularly those with learning problems. The occasion can be seen as information-giving or information-getting, or a mixture of both. Those who would accept it as an opportunity for parents to offer judgements on the school are probably a tiny minority.

Indeed, some teachers undoubtedly view the event with trepidation: those who are young and childless may fear the older and more experienced parent; others are afraid their professional knowledge will be challenged with questions they cannot answer; some may be concerned that their teaching methods will not meet with approval, while others may be apprehensive that they may be blamed for the child's failure to make progress.

Other teachers – more confident or experienced at handling interviews – often centre their attention on how efficiently and quickly they can 'process' the parents and some even take great pride in being the first member of staff to complete the list and escape to the nearest pub!

THE PARENT'S VIEWPOINT

But what of the parents – what do they make of these meetings, how useful do they find them, what are they actually coming for, and what expectations do they have?

It's a chance so see what the teacher's like, you know, this person she's always talking about at home.

It's really just to confirm what we already know, to make sure that in school she's the same as we see her at home.

I think we go, well, to show the teacher that we're interested in the kid, basically ... because if they are willing to give the time up to show us that they are interested, I think it's only fair that we reciprocate by making an effort to go and see the teacher.

Open Days are really the only time, the only opportunity for parents to go and see what is happening and what the children are doing, you know, and take a close look at books and so on.

We come because it shows interest and is an incentive to the child to work.

We expect to find out how she's doing and how we can help.

So parents also have different purposes in mind as they prepare to attend an interview. Some want to see the teacher in order to assess him or her as a person; they will listen to the way the talk is conducted and look for the attitudes such talk reveals, rather than attend to the content of what is said. Others want specific information on their children's performance and will listen very carefully to the spoken word. There are those who place little value on talking on the teacher at all but who want to look at the classroom, the displays and the children's work. Others come expecting specific discussion on ways to help their child with a problem they have already identified. Some go simply to stop themselves being labelled apathetic or uncaring, while others would rather not come at all as the event has nothing to offer them that a written report could not provide.

Moreover, parents view the consultation with mixed feelings. Some, with unhappy memories of their own schooling, are afraid of appearing ignorant or worry that they will be baffled by the teacher's language; some believe that if

Dear

Thank you for your support.

Your time to see me is   Monday 15 November/Wednesday 17 November/Thursday 18

November at _____ p.m.

I would like to talk with you about   progress so far in 2J
and what I expect her/him to do during the rest of the time in my class.

Would you like to make a note here of the things you'd like to talk with me
about?

_____

_____

_____

dear mum and dad will you
come to are assembly at ++past
ten coffee and bissuit are
served at 31st march you can
look round school

from RICHARD

Monday
Workshop.

Come in on Monday afternoons
to make books for the children
to work in.

Help to mount the children's
art work.

Cut out letters for displays

and lots more!

Wednesday.   انگریزی سیکھیے

انگریزی زبان نہ صرف انگلستان کی موجودہ زبان ہے ۔ بلکہ
یہ بہت سی اقوامی زبان قرار دی گئی ہے ۔ اس کا بولنا ، لکھنا اور
پڑھنا سیکھنا نہ صرف آپ کے لیے فائدہ مند ہے بلکہ آپ اپنی
منزلی کی بھی نئی طرح سے مدد کر سکتی ہیں ۔ کیا آپ ان باتوں
سے متفق ہیں؟ تو پھر یہ آپ کے لیے سنہری موقع ہے کہ
"بلوبیل بل سکول" میں انگریزی سیکھانے کا انتظام کیا گیا ہے ۔
آپ اپنا نام علیحدہ کیرونیٹی شیمبر کر دیں ۔ بلکے آپ اپنی سہیلیوں
کو بھی ساتھ لائیں ۔   شکریہ ۔

they really speak their minds their child will suffer reprisals; those who know there are problems may feel guilty or embarrassed and fear what they are going to hear; others are suspicious of particular teaching methods and, concerned that their child's future is at stake, may be anxious or aggressive; boredom, scepticism or cynicism may well predominate amongst those parents who feel the talk is valueless or that the whole occasion is a charade.

Both parties to the encounter, then, have very varied attitudes and perspectives on it and the way they handle the occasion will reflect this. Teachers may possibly talk most of the time to prevent the awkward question, or take refuge in generalities and platitudes to avoid conflict or disagreement. Parents may become defensive or very voluble or may do no more than politely listen and go away with their real concerns undisclosed.

TEACHER–PARENT INTERVIEWS: SOME PRACTICAL IDEAS TO CONSIDER

Any careful examination of parents evenings, designed to bring about their improvement and based upon examination of what actually takes place, is likely to uncover a number of recurring themes. Differences of perspective and experience between teachers and parents are exacerbated by an apparent conspiracy of silence about the actual and potential purposes of such meetings. The tables on pages 76–77 summarize the range of possibilities here. Obviously greater progress could be made if the reasons for such meetings were clear and agreed by both teachers and parents.

Whilst it is useful to examine a parent's evening as an important event in a school's programme, it is also necessary to consider them as part of a continuing process, in which teacher–parent relationships are defined in important ways and 'managed', and through which parents come to make judgements about their children's schooling. It is also a major opportunity in the home–school programme to focus upon the efforts and achievements of individual pupils.

The following practical suggestions, drawn from our work with teachers, add up to something of a basic strategy for reviewing this important aspect of home–school relations and could well serve as the starting point for a wider and fuller examination of a school's efforts in this area.

- Get parents evenings put on the agenda of the next school staff meeting. Home–school matters are hardly ever raised as a legitimate area for discussion and teacher development.
- Make sure that invitations make the purpose of the interviews clear. Better still, send out an invitation that sets up a 'two way agenda'. This gives teachers an opportunity to declare the particular things they want to raise with a child's parents. It also gives parents the same opportunity to identify issues that *they* want to discuss with teachers.
- Record the 'Questions parents ask'. Not only does this remind teachers that parents have a right to ask questions – it might even get teachers to listen a bit! Sometimes the questions that have been written down reveal useful patterns of concern and important variations of need that can be acted upon.

Is it really true that teachers 'never see the parents that they most want to see?' Why do some parents not attend parents' evenings? What can or should be done about this? What kinds of 'evidence' can be provided to stimulate discussion

Table 3.4: Parent–teacher interviews – school and parental purposes

---

School purposes

To inform parents of the child's progress

To meet demands for accountability

To establish and maintain good relations with parents

To share with the parent the problems and difficulties the child has in school

To explain and justify the school's policies and decisions as they affect individual pupils

To critically review with the parent the child's experience of schooling

To learn more about the child from the parent's perspective

To learn more about parental opinions on what the school is doing

To identify areas of tension and disagreement

To identify ways in which parents can help their children

To negotiate jointly decisions about the child's education

Parental purposes

To get a report on the child's progress

To identify any problem

To confirm existing judgements

To find out ways of helping the child

To see the child's work and possibly compare it with that of other children

To meet the people who teach the child

To bring up problems identified at home

To learn more about the school and the teaching

To inform the teacher about a particular matter

To question the teacher about issues of concern

Table 3.5: Parent–teacher consultation – a framework for identifying issues and questions

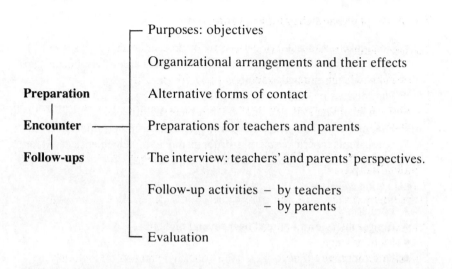

Preparation
|
Encounter
|
Follow-ups

— Purposes: objectives

Organizational arrangements and their effects

Alternative forms of contact

Preparations for teachers and parents

The interview: teachers' and parents' perspectives.

Follow-up activities – by teachers
– by parents

— Evaluation

Table 3.6: Parent–teacher interviews – some questions

1. What are parents' evenings for? Are there different kinds of purpose?
2. What organizational arrangements do you make? What are the effects of these arrangements?
3. What other kinds of preparation are made?
4. What actually happens on a parents evening?
5. What influences the size of turnout and the 'quality' of the evening?
6. What do parents and teachers really get out of such an evening? Does this vary? According to what? Do you have any evidence to support this?
7. What kinds of record do you have of (a) individual consultations and (b) general issues that arise from the evening?
8. What kinds of follow-up can (a) teachers, and (b) parents carry out? Do you have any evidence that this happens?
9. Do you know of other schools that tackle parent–teacher consultation differently to your school? Give brief outlines.
10. What seem to you to be:
    (i) the main strengths and weaknesses of your general approach to consultation, and
    (ii) those areas that seem ready for growth and development, or require to be changed?

Table 3.7: Teacher–parent consultation

Constructive suggestions for schools and teachers

GETTING A CLEARER PICTURE: CRITICAL REVIEW

- Undertake an honest, critical review of present arrangements. Look for evidence. Identify different parental prespectives and views. Locate gaps in knowledge and undestanding
- Staff discussion –aims and objectives
- Examine invitations sent out. Are they clear, helpful etc.?
- Examine organizational arrangements and discuss their effects – is this how parents experience them? – different modes of judgement catered for?
- Alternative arrangements and kinds of experiences

Organizational changes

- Format
- Longer interviews – spread over several nights
- More privacy
- Different times of day
- Appointments: non appointments

Arrangements for those who don't come

- New dates or appointments
- Home visits for some
- Special hand-written letter
- Special arrangements, e.g. home–school diaries

Different modes of consultation

- Based on child's work (in class or sent home previously with explanatory note)
- Based on written report or pupil diary etc.
- Based on questions previously identified by teachers and/or parents
- Incorporating prepared checklists

Alternative forms of organization

- Open house – 'contract'. No fixed dates. Two visits per term
- Regular 'at home' or surgery sessions at regular times
- Contact in different, out-of-school venues, e.g. village halls etc.

Guidelines for staff

- Do they exist? Need improving?
- Keep a record of the informal contacts initiated both by parents and the school.
- Are there patterns here?

continued overleaf

Table 3.7: Continued

- SOME SUGGESTIONS FOR NEXT TIME
- Look especially at teacher preparations for next parents evening
- Make folder containing typical cross section of a child's work in that class. Think about displays of work – brief, lively handout of a topic of current concern or stage of development etc.
- Arrange to keep written records during evening
  i) Questions parents ask
  ii) Notes on individual children
- Arrange follow-up meeting for staff to discuss – general action
                                         – particular cases
- Use consultation evenings to identify practical things that tachers, parents and pupils can do after the evening on an individual basis
- Teacher-prepared notes or suggestions to do as follow-ups
- Fixing 'targets' for individual pupils
- Teachers feeding information into the system as appropriate

SOME SMALL-SCALE INNOVATIONS

- Meeting parents as a class group
- As above, to describe forthcoming work and seek specific kinds of help
- Home diaries on a small-scale experimental basis
- Using pupils as mediators of their work with their parents
- Involving pupils in the consultation process
- Linking consultation with other curricular activities, e.g. exhibitions, events, working demonstrations, etc.
- 'Open house' or 'Contracts' as alternative form of contact
- 'Take-aways' containing suggestions for parental help, 'joint learning tasks', home projects etc.
- Tape-slide sequence or video-film etc., depicting 'A typical week in the classroom'.

SOME LONGER-TERM DEVELOPMENTS

- Arrange Staff Development Programme around activities that
  – generally sensitize staff to issues, parental perspectives etc.
  – tackle identified, specific topics.
  – disseminate good ideas and practices from individuals throughout the staff
- Let parents know that you want and value their views in this area
  – Write to them
  – Air the matter at the PTA
  – Ask parents informally on appropriate occasions etc.
- Tackle 'The parents that don't turn up' as a separate, important issue. Possible trial use of some home visits as an alternative
- Special consideration of the needs and problems of the new, inexperienced teacher
- Harnessing a parent's interest in their own child and extending it to a consideration of wider issues.

about the work that children are doing, not only for parents' evenings, but generally. Are there also opportunities for parents to examine, observe and, above all, to experience the kinds of tasks that their children are given in class? It can be useful for both teachers and parents to think of face to face interviews as part of a process. The accompanying chart, provides a framework of questions to facilitate this and might be used as the basis of a discussion.

Is it possible to have a genuine teacher–parent–child triangle, as is often advocated in the rhetoric of home and school relations, without directly involving children and young people in the process of consultation? There are some interesting developments in this area, involving children of different ages. It is also the proposal that is likely to divide teachers most deeply.

A number of years ago, I worked with a group of teachers and headteachers who had chosen, following earlier work on written communication, to look at teacher–parent interviews as a key example of face to face contact. During the course of our work we were able to identify and try out a wide range of practical ideas. These are reproduced here, without comment, as many teachers have found them useful.

Looking back, these suggestions seem to incorporate three overlapping strategies, which are made explicit here as they may also be useful for examining other forms of home–school practice. They embody, in an undifferentiated way, the idea that:

i) Teacher–parent interviews as we know them, can become more effective with suitable modification and reform. Such a view tends to stress improvements in timing, location and organization – in improving the quality of the arrangements that are made.

ii) Existing models are no longer of value and should be scrapped altogether and replaced with something different, such as an informal arrangement to meet an agreed contract or very different forms of contact.

iii) Teacher–parent interviews should not be considered on their own, in isolation, but as part of a wider approach which stresses a number of options and alternatives and which also tries to take into account the different needs of parents for information and evidence (see Chapter 3: How Parents make Judgements).

Parents and the Curriculum

Several years ago, we decided that the time had come to take an in-service initiative in our work in home–school relations that focused firmly on curriculum matters. There were a number of reasons for the timing of this, but mainly that (a) school curricula had become an object of widespread public attention and concern, amongst politicians and professionals alike; (b) our extensive programme of home interviews with parents had revealed that there was considerable anxiety across all kinds of background and experience about what children were learning, and especially about how they were being taught. Many parents felt that because they didn't know or understand what was going on in classrooms they were unable to help their children at home; (c) because of advances in home–school thinking and practice, greater emphasis needed to be given to the job of developing home–school links that focused upon children's learning

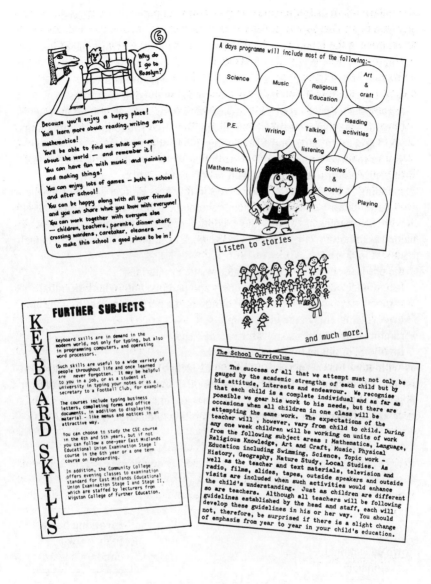

⑥

Why do I go to Rosslyn?

Because you'll enjoy a happy place!
You'll learn more about reading, writing and mathematics!
You'll be able to find out what you can about the world — and remember it!
You can have fun with music and painting and making things!
You can enjoy lots of games — both in school and after school!
You can be happy along with all your friends and you can share what you know with everyone!
You can work together with everyone else — children, teachers, parents, dinner staff, crossing wardens, caretaker, cleaners — to make this school a good place to be in!

A days programme will include most of the following:—

Science · Music · Religious Education · Art & craft · P.E. · Writing · Talking & listening · Reading activities · Mathematics · Stories & poetry · Playing

Listen to stories

and much more.

FURTHER SUBJECTS

KEYBOARD SKILLS

Keyboard skills are in demand in the modern world, not only for typing, but also in programming computers, and operating word processors.

Such skills are useful to a wide variety of people throughout life and once learned are never forgotten. It may be helpful to you in a job, or as a student at university in typing your notes or as a secretary to a Football Club, for example.

The courses include typing business letters, completing forms and office documents, in addition to displaying material - like menus and notices in an attractive way.

You can choose to study the CSE course in the 4th and 5th years, but if not you can follow a one-year East Midlands Educational Union Examination Stage I course in the 6th year or a one term course on Keyboarding.

In addition, the Community College offers evening classes to examination standard for East Midlands Educational Union Examination Stage I and Stage II, which are staffed by lecturers from Wigston College of Further Education.

The School Curriculum.

The success of all that we attempt must not only be gauged by the academic strengths of each child but by his attitude, interests and endeavour. We recognise that each child is a complete individual and as far as possible we gear his work to his needs, but there are occasions when all children in one class will be attempting the same work. The expectations of the teacher will, however, vary from child to child. During any one week children will be working on units of work from the following subject areas : Mathematics, Language, Religious Knowledge, Art and Craft, Music, Physical Education including Swimming, Science, Topic work - History, Geography, Nature Study, Local Studies. As well as the teacher and text materials, television and radio, films, slides, tapes, outside speakers and outside visits are included when such activities would enhance the child's understanding. Just as children are different so are teachers. Although all teachers will be following guidelines established by the head and staff, each will develop these guidelines in his or her way. You should not, therefore, be surprised if there is a slight change of emphasis from year to year in your child's education.

– the central task of schools and the basis of a genuinely educational partnership between teachers and parents.

To launch this initiative, we chose the following extract from one of our parent interviews, which still seems to put its finger on a central ambivalence and contradiction that lies at the heart of home–school relationships:

> at this particular school, they like you to be involved in the things they do at school, but as far as your child's work and things like that are concerned, I think they like you to leave that to them. They like you to join in with things, you know, erm, anything that's going off at school – sport and all that – you're involved in all that, but the actual work that the child does, I think they just prefer to tell you their bit . . . (Parent)

Responding to the issues they perceived in this quotation, a group of teachers went on to identify lines of practical development in five areas. Interestingly enough, these areas have, with the exception of the involvement of pupils, remained as important concerns both in the work of schools generally and in their treatment in this book. They consist of:

the production of curriculum related written materials;

face to face contact between teachers and parents, both with individual
   parents and with the parents of children in a particular class as a group;

involving parents in the classroom;

running curriculum sessions for parents; and

involving pupils in home–school work.

As with other major concerns in the home–school area, parental communication and involvement which focuses on the curriculum can serve a range of overlapping purposes, with their associated issues and characteristic practices, which serve as the basis of an agenda for both planning and action (Figure 3.6).

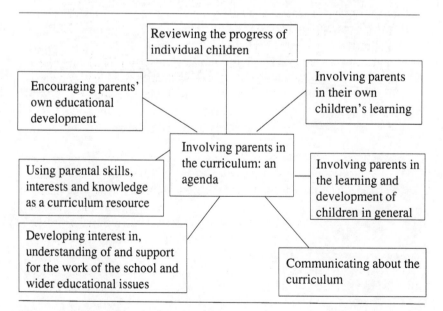

Figure 3.6: Involving parents in the curriculum – an agenda

Table 3.7: Parent and school orientated action

Parent orientated action	School orientated action
Parental concern for their own children.	Wider interest in the education and development of children generally.
Parental perspectives and experience as parents.	Turns parents into 'surrogate' teachers. The 'professionalization' of parents.
Meeting parents' own social and educational needs.	Responding to the expressed needs of schools and pupils.
The interests and concerns of the parents of the school's children as a whole	Working with relatively small numbers of 'sponsored' parents.
Located in the home setting.	Located in the school setting.

This agenda also incorporates a number of recurring themes which serve as a healthy reminder of the different perspectives of teachers and parents, as well as drawing attention to alternative tasks and courses of action, as shown in Table 3.7.

There is, given the complexity of the agenda, an enormous range of opportunities and practices for home–school cooperation in this area. To make life manageable, I have chosen three main areas to show this range and to provide a number of illustrations of issues and practical examples:

1. Parents working in schools and classrooms;
2. Running a curriculum session for parents;
3. Home helps!

The section is completed by a very brief look at a number of interesting recent developments which focus upon the twin tasks of communicating with parents about the curriculum and involving them in their children's learning.

Parents working in schools and classrooms

As elsewhere, it is extremely useful to identify the distinctive purposes and agendas that parents and teachers have for working together on school premises. Some of these will be shared, pointing to the basis for some productive joint initiatives; others will be contradictory, needing to be brought into the open to tackle tensions or find practical compromises; yet others will reflect the distinctive purposes and concerns of the two groups that can, if acknowledged, be exploited constructively. So, being clear about what teachers and parents expect and hope to get out of the arrangement provides a realistic basis for tailoring activities to meet both sets of needs and circumstances and attempts to maximize their effectiveness.

A SCHOOL'S REASONS FOR SEEKING PARENTAL HELP

As a means of improving home–school relationships
　　Getting to know some parents better, through cooperative activity.
　　Showing them how things are done, so improving the quality of their interest and giving it a more practical focus.
　　Raising the profile of educational tasks and processes generally.
Schools need the active support of their parents
　　To endorse their general approach
　　To share both the responsibility and the task of educating their children.
　　To tackle special problems and particular ventures.
　　To identify ways in which they (parents) can help their children learn.
Schools need a hand with many aspects of their work
　　Schools need – especially these days – extra pairs of hands to help in classrooms and around the school.
　　Parents can help in ways that free teachers to do other things, which they might not otherwise be able to do.
　　Extra adults can enhance the quality of a school's provision by giving some children individual attention or helping to sustain small group work.
Parental knowledge, interests and experience are valuable resources for the school
　　These resources are available in many forms – directly in person, through talk and materials or via contacts. (Some schools keep this information systematically, as a kind of inventory.)
　　They can be used across the curriculum as a source of potent learning, as 'teaching' input or as a means of broadening the curriculum.

SOME PRACTICAL EXAMPLES

Giving individual attention to pupils
　　Hearing children read (including the more fluent readers who can be overlooked).
　　Using flashcards.
　　Help with spelling and writing.
　　Extra opportunities for discussion with adults.
　　Coaching individuals in sporting activities.
　　Special help with disruptive child.
　　Help with computer work.
Routine tasks to free teacher
　　Preparing displays of work.
　　Typing children's stories as reading materials.
　　Establishing contacts for local visits.
　　Helping in libraries and resource centres.
　　Stimulating interest in play with younger children.
　　Helping groups with weighing, measuring and counting activities.
　　Recording stories, poems and nursery rhymes.
　　Repairing equipment and materials.
　　Being on a rota as nursery helpers.
　　Running the school bookshop.

Utilizing parental skills and experience
> Teaching dancing and music.
> Running craft and hobbies groups, e.g. pottery, cookery, photography.
> Careers talks (my job), giving job interviews.
> Cycling Proficiency courses.
> Umpiring, refereeing, coaching.
> Making puppets, stage scenery.
> 'Living history' – local studies, social change etc.
> Using Asian and West Indian parents for ethnic cookery and for telling stories in their own languages.

SOME REASONS WHY PARENTS VOLUNTEER TO HELP IN SCHOOLS AND CLASSROOMS

To help their own children
> Indirectly, through better relationships with teachers.
> By becoming more familiar with the school's curriculum and its way of doing things.
> By identifying practical forms of help for their own children.

To help the school
> With a variety of tasks, some of which may relate directly or indirectly to their own children.
> To provide additional support and general practical help, in exchange for the satisfactions that derive from it.
> To take over some responsibilities, in order to free teachers to do other things more effectively.

To meet some of their own needs
> To meet educational needs, both latent and conscious.
> For the satisfaction of doing interesting and worthwhile jobs.
> To meet other parents, in a lively, sociable setting.
> To get a wider experience of working with children.
> To feel useful, valued and needed.

Often schools (particularly primary schools) which attempt to meet some of these parental needs as well as their own, will develop an extensive and wide-ranging programme of activities of mutual benefit. This is often accompanied by the provision of a parents room, which symbolizes the participation and involvement of parents, as well as providing a base where parents can meet and relax or carry out some of the tasks they have come in for. Parents' rooms can vary enormously in the facilities they offer and in the uses made of them. They can be lively social centres, up-to-date information and resource centres or busy workrooms. Many parents' rooms are, however, extremely basic, uninviting and apparently suffering from rigor mortis! I have the impression that there is much still to be tried out and learned about the role of such provision in our schools.

There is another issue raised by the practice of involving parents in these ways. Plenty of schools, particularly in the pre-school and primary sectors, have extensive experience of using parents as a source of additional help and support for hard-pressed teachers in the classroom; a number have begun to develop something of a strategy for exploiting the educative potential of such help, but only a few have been able to come to terms with the longer-term problems of continuing parental participation (a problem that is characteristic of home–school links generally).

Parents may be quite happy to carry out routine and mundane tasks as a way of breaking the ice and getting used to life in classrooms. For some, this will continue to be alright. Their satisfaction may come, for example, from mixing with other parents in a setting where there is always something going on. But there are others who, as their confidence grows and their interest deepens, are likely to seek more demanding forms of involvement and different satisfactions. They will also want to see the point of what they are being asked to do.

Such issues, which stem from the dynamic nature of parental involvement raise matters that also involve the professional development of teachers which, for most schools, has meant learning on their feet. This is one of several examples in this account, of the way in which opening-up schools and classrooms will inevitably bring the kind of problems as well as satisfactions which, sooner or later, will have to be faced.

Running a curriculum evening

Running a curriculum evening of one kind or another has gradually become a feature of many home–school programmes. The planning and preparation for such an event will require considerable time and effort and there will inevitably be a certain amount of apprehension about how the evening will turn out. Consequently, it is worth giving some thought to what kind of session is thought to be most relevant and beneficial to parents and teachers at that time.

Such a session can have many different kinds of focus, from whole school issues and policies to work in particular curriculum areas, from the introduction of new courses to the examination of established areas where new approaches have been introduced. I have chosen to illustrate the last of these, for reasons which will be made clear, although the issues and principles would be much the same in each case.

A maths or reading evening can potentially attract a lot of support, for both are regarded as basic curriculum areas, by teachers and parents alike; they are also the focus of much public interest and anxiety. Often negative attitudes towards the teaching of reading or maths can be traced to parents' own experience as pupils and to tensions which arise from the doing of homework and the frustration of parents in being unable to provide adequate help. So a maths or reading evening, if successful, can be an excellent way of enlisting the active help of parents in their children's learning. It is a good focus for a discussion of teaching methods and for a constructive examination of the value of combining traditional and modern ways of organizing learning.

Such an evening can take very different forms and provide very different degrees of satisfaction for both teachers and parents. It is noticeable, however, that more enthusiasm seems to be shown for events that are thoughtfully planned and carefully organized; friendly, but purposeful; down to earth and practical (rather than exploring general issues) and, above all, the common denominator of a successful evening seems to combine opportunities to see, to discuss and to do − in short, to *experience*.

SOME PRACTICAL SUGGESTIONS

Be ambitious without going over the top! There are a number of possibilities which can be combined in different ways:

    video, tape or slide presentation

    demonstration lessons

    informal discussion

    small group tasks and activities etc.

If many parents want to come, it may be better to run the evening twice (or for different year groups or ages). Try to have as many staff as possible to take part and who are ready to explain policy and practice. Don't be afraid to organize part of the evening in small groups. The extra involvement that this brings almost guarantees success. But don't use Brownie Patrol Leader tactics to do this! Try to include some tasks and materials that parents will be familiar with, as well as stuff that is new. Don't have too much that is strange. Allow at least a term to plan the session, to allow time for setting-up exhibitions, trying out small group tasks etc. Use 'experts' with caution. In particular, make sure that: they are likely to be good communicators with an audience of parents, especially when it is large and very mixed; that they are not either laying down the law or acting as your mouthpiece, but supplementing the work of the school. Never let one or two individuals with strong opinions dominate the proceedings. Everyone else will switch off if this happens.

Many parents would find it useful to have materials to take away and examine at leisure. These might include: copies of the syllabus or scheme of work; examples of the pupil's record sheet; things children can do with their parents at home; information about relevant publications of interest to parents; and, an invitation to make an appointment to come to the school and discuss further any of these materials, or the issues they raise. Don't ruin a good evening with a plenary session that is long-winded or unproductive. Most people will have had plenty of opportunity to express opinions and ask questions during the evening. Try to listen to what parents are saying and respond constructively to it. Recent research has uncovered many areas where teachers could usefully tackle areas of parental interest, anxiety and concern (e.g. topic work, computer studies) to their mutual benefit and in the interests of their children. Have a short meeting with colleagues a day or two after the session to evaluate what has been learned from the experience and plan how that can be utilized in other parts of the home–school programme. Here, as elsewhere, build on success and positive experience!

Home helps!

The issue of contact with parents in their own homes, most obviously through the practice of home visits, is one that appears to divide teacher opinion deeply. There are plenty of teachers, for example, (including a number who are otherwise sympathetic to home–school work, who see such contact as falling clearly beyond the boundaries of a teacher's job and his or her competence and as a corresponding invasion of the privacy of parents and families.

Then there are others for whom contact with children's homes is legitimate – even desirable – but fraught with practical difficulties in the shape of inflexible staffing arrangements or genuine competition from other priorities in the home–school programme and elsewhere.

Finally, there is a steadily growing number of teachers for whom such activities are an important and perfectly natural part of any active educational partnership between families and schools. For them, the demands of time and energy that are required are compensated for by the kind of relationship and professional understanding that is very difficult to achieve in any other way.

In this section, however, home visiting is seen as only one of several forms of contact involving families in their own setting, and as a means to wider ends:

HOME VISITS

Current practice stems from visits undertaken for widely-differing purposes:
- to get to know a new family;
- to follow-up a particular concern generated at school by referring to a child's family circumstances;
- as a response to previous repeated failure to establish contact through the other forms of communication;
- to set up, or to introduce, home-based projects and schemes, which require the active interest of parents.

HOME–SCHOOL DIARIES, TWO-WAY REPORTS

These are well-established practices, particularly in the field of special needs, where regular and detailed practical cooperation is crucial. Their main purposes are: to establish a two-way communication system, built around joint tasks and responsibilities and monitor its subsequent development; and, to identify the kind of information that schools can utilize in the classroom, in remedial or other ways.

SKILLS FOR THE ACTIVE INVOLVEMENT OF PARENTS IN THEIR CHILDREN'S LEARNING

There are plenty of powerful examples here, particularly in the early years and special needs areas. The most spectacular, however, has grown from the involvement of parents in their children's reading, drawing upon deservedly well-known schemes around the country. Such developments have done more to justify previous acts of faith and to convert the sceptic, than any other single activity in the history of home–school relations. There are now a number of available, down to earth accounts of how such work can be undertaken. The important question at this stage concerns the extent to which such involvement can effectively be harnessed to other areas of the curriculum and to other classroom activities, with similar results.

HOME TASKS

These are definitely *not* the same as homework, as is generally known and resented by parents and pupils everywhere! Home tasks, or joint learning tasks: utilize the home and neighbourhood as an educative environment; can extend the classroom into the child's out-of-school life; and, can root classroom activities in children's everyday home experience or use it as a starting point for inquiry work.

To be really effective, however, the development of joint tasks needs to be especially sensitive to the physical and cultural dimensions of social life in the community and to the widely varying circumstances of children's lives.

SOME EXAMPLES

Listed below are some examples of observing, measuring and recording activities based in the home and the immediate vicinity.
  • Language-based games and activities
  • Environmental topics and activities
  • The science of everyday life
  • Making things, collecting things, describing things, classifying things
  • Undertaking various kinds of research, involving family and neighbourhood history etc.

Such curriculum themes can, with a little imagination, (a) yield a wide range of stimulating tasks and activities, which are accessible to children of widely-differing ages and abilities; (b) offer the prospect of a relevant but educationally demanding and progressive curriculum; (c) be used both to initiate work that will be developed later in the classroom and to provide opportunities to enrich, develop and supplement classroom-based work; and (d) make the curriculum more visible to parents, in ways that make more sense than conventional homework, often tapping *their* knowledge and experience and inviting their cooperation and development.

Class-based parents' meetings or joint newsletters (see page 88) provide a useful opportunity to get feedback on this kind of activity, to introduce new tasks for the coming term and to iron out any problems or difficulties that parents might anticipate in lending their support.

Some recent developments

In this section I have tried to sketch in a number of lines of practical development that are emerging, taking root and likely to spread. There is no attempt to do this comprehensively, but rather in a way that suggests a variety of current issues, new focal points of organization and different ways of working. The selection made, however, does reveal a number of interesting similarities and points of growth and development.

In the first place, these recent developments often illustrate a number of new and wider influences upon the education service. The use of parents' group meetings, based on the class or tutor group, for example, owes a great deal to a growing awareness of the structure and form of home–school relations in other EEC countries, based largely upon the work of Alistair Macbeth. Such a comparative perspective taps different bodies of legislation, tradition and experience, revealing important areas of similarity and differences of approach. So, although home–school practice is generally less well developed in most EEC member states than it is in Britain, the class meeting – held to explain the coming term's work – is a well established feature that is worth looking at and considering as a suitable case for adoption, with necessary modification.

So, too, the growing use of video in our schools owes as much, if not more, to the increasing interest in and adoption of its use on the domestic front as in the education service. In both of these arenas, however, I have the impression that its present uses are rather limited and restricted compared with its potential for creative use and active learning, amongst children and adults alike.

There is a view of educational development which sees the future almost entirely in terms of the extension of what already exists, or of 'more of the same'. Most of the examples in this section, by contrast, break away from such a view, to illustrate rather different kinds of ground rules and basic assumptions. These differences are represented here by family sessions, which can have important repercussions for the alteration of basic attitudes towards learner roles and family relationships, with significant ripple effects for all those involved.

In a similar way, the actual practical forms that reciprocal home–school obligations and responsibilities might take are being significantly influenced in England and Wales by the influence of politically-led legislation. As with much legislation in areas characterized by widely-differing attitudes and experience such legislation, giving rise, for example, to the requirement of the 1986 Act for an annual report and parents meeting, does tend to be rather unclear about the nature of practical outcomes. It certainly represents, however, fundamental changes in the relationships between 'providers' and 'consumers'. Nowhere is this more sharply encountered than in the recent attempts to develop a viable form of home–school 'contract', which is currently being explored by at least one professional association, several LEAs and a number of individual schools.

As well as demonstrating a number of new and wider influences and different ground rules, current developments in home–school practice reinforce and serve as a general reminder of a number of familiar problems. Trying to develop home–school activity is not 'just' a matter of developing more supportive attitudes, but of finding appropriate organizational forms and, above all, calls for the development of new knowledge and skills. Working with adults, for example, makes demands for which initial training and previous experience are unlikely to have made any useful contribution

The class meeting

As has been suggested, arrangements involving the parents of children in their class or tutor group getting together as a group, are part of established practice in the United States and in a number of European countries. Such a practice seems to represent enormous, undeveloped potential as a focus for home–school activity. It is able, for example, to reconcile some of the sharp differences between: arrangements that are based upon the needs, concerns and experience of individual families and their members, most characteristically embodied in parents' evenings, school reports and impromptu visits by anxious parents; and, arrangements that focus upon the representation of parent views and experience as a body, their shared needs and common concerns and the development of a wider interest in, and involvement with the life and work of the school as a whole. The class meeting can serve a range of different functions, or specialize and give emphasis to some of these in the following ways.

PROVIDING A BASIC UNIT IN THE ORGANIZATION OF HOME–SCHOOL ACTIVITY

This is more personal and accessible than many home–school events and activities in:

- Helping parents to get to know each other
- Reinforcing and reviewing the effectiveness of the school's basic arrangements for communication and involvement, on a user-friendly scale and seeking their honest views.
- Identifying and electing class or form parent representatives to link up with school-wide groups, on the one hand, and with particular neighbourhoods on the other, to ensure that different communities are represented.
- Building up an inventory of parental knowledge, interests, skill and experience, to tap in a variety of ways.

ENLISTING THE ACTIVE SUPPORT AND INVOLVEMENT OF PARENTS IN THEIR CHILDREN'S WORK

- Reviewing recent work and identifying areas of parental action which could be remedial, reinforcing or enriching.
- Seeking parental involvement at a practical level, both through voluntary activity in school and through helping their children at home.
- Exploring the work of the coming term or year, putting parents in the picture and suggesting possible areas for mutual support and involvement between parents and teachers.

LAUNCHING SPECIAL PROJECTS AND PROGRAMMES OF WORK

Such as the introduction of new courses or approaches, parental involvement in reading schemes etc.

TACKLING COMMON PROBLEMS AND SHARED CONCERNS

This includes those that relate to school life and work, e.g. doing homework, and project work; and those that are characteristic of the age or stage of development and school career of children of that particular age, for example, discipline problems, and sex education.

The educational use of video in home–school relations

The use of video remains potentially exciting, but relatively unexplored, both as a medium of communication and as a tool for learning – for adults and children alike, for video is relatively cheap, reliable, flexible and easy to use. This contrasts markedly with the impression I have (unsupported by any systematic evidence) that schools currently use video only to play back pre-recorded material or to record significant events and occasions in the life of the school, as a kind of visual, but passive chronicle for parental consumption.

In an earlier section, considerable emphasis was given to examples of written communication and face to face contact as constituting the most basic, enduring forms of home–school communication. Against this background, the use of video serves to mitigate some of the more obvious weaknesses and limitations of these basic forms, as well as providing a new range of options and alternatives.

Finally, the imaginative use of video can provide an important window on the life and work of the school, enabling many parents to participate, often in a vivid and detailed way and play a significant part in the development of their understanding of educational processes and institutions.

SOME USES OF VIDEO

- To inform parents about the life and work of the school
- As a visual prospectus for new parents.
- To chronicle aspects of school life and record special events.
- To provide a catalyst for a discussion of educational issues of concern to many parents, e.g. classroom life and organization; innovations and developments; and problems to tackle from specially produced video materials.
- To provide prepared tapes for parents to use at home, in connection with parents' role as educators; supporting the work of the school; and, 'training' films for parents to borrow using language games, home-based learning etc.
- To provide an educational tool for parents to use in exploring aspects of the life and work of the school from their own perspectives and on their own terms; and, to express and explore their own ideas and experience, as a vehicle of their educational development.

While these represent some of the more obvious types of use, there are many other possibilities, such as: (1) Staff development materials, based on existing events and activities that involve parents or parent groups. These might include the recording of actual events, as well as simulated activities for analysis and discussion. (2) Diagnostic materials, produced in school, or jointly with parents, both as a record of individual progress and as a guide to remedial action and support. Currently such material is most likely to be found in the education of children with special needs, although there is no reason why this should remain so. (3) Using pre-recorded programmes on educational topics as a way of raising the consciousness and leading the discussion of contemporary issues and concerns. Examples include television series about schools, made for parents, special 'one-offs' on burning issues such as the 1988 Act, or the opportunity for parents to preview material that will later be shown to pupils

Family sessions

Although not particularly widespread, family sessions have often achieved spectacularly successful results. I know, for example, of one early evening maths workshop that has regularly attracted between 80 and 100 children and parents over several years. How can such a pattern – which strikingly contradicts the experience of many pupils and their long-suffering parents – be explained?

Family sessions owe much to two overlapping educational beliefs, translated into practical action. The first stems from the view, linked to positive experience, which sees children not as self-contained learning machines, but inextricably linked to their families and neighbourhoods. In spite of the rhetoric (see Chapter 4) parents and pupils are usually treated by schools and teachers as separate constituent parts, creating different problems and calling for different kinds of recognition and response. Family sessions, by definition, tap directly into the educational needs and experiences of *families*.

The second element derives from the growing experience of community schools and community education and their increasing willingness to develop flexible attitudes and arrangements that are more responsive to the lives and circumstances of learners of all types, ages and backgrounds. Such an approach has resulted in shared daytime classes, informal styles of adult education and family sessions.

For present purposes family sessions are characterized by a sense of shared purpose and by a flexibility of teaching, learning and support roles within family groups, varying according to purpose and circumstance. So, in a 'family maths' session, for instance, parents may become participants by adopting a role which suggests active remedial support for their children, within a framework of professional leadership and guidance. But the roles can just as easily be reversed, here as elsewhere, with children providing support for their *parents'* learning. There are many areas, such as computing or languages where children and young people can start or move ahead of their parents, or where increased motivation and interest gives them an edge. In other cases, where families attempt to develop new interests, knowledge and skills 'from scratch', family statuses can get turned on their head, with interesting consequences for existing relationships.

So, family sessions can serve a range of purposes and needs, such as remedial, supplementary or enrichment activities for parents as well as pupils which relate to the main curriculum provision of the school; joint activities and shared interests that are fun, but no respecters of age and experience, e.g. games such as chess, computing, much art and music work, and many hobbies and leisure interests; and the development of new knowledge, interests and skills, that serve shared family concerns, e.g. family holidays, community projects etc.

The representation of parental views and experience as a collective body

This topic, more than any other in the book, is subject to the contradictions and ambivalences of the author's own views, prejudices and experiences in this area. For whilst I can see clearly that there is a need for parental views and experience to be represented collectively and, on occasions, formally, I have much less confidence about some of the existing ways in which this is being done and in a number of current reforms that are about to be implemented.

This ambivalence and scepticism is strongly grounded in my own experience, both as a parent and a professional, in involvement with my own children's Parent–Teacher Associations (PTA), in working with a wide range of parent groups

and bodies and from periods of office on school governing bodies, as an elected
parent representative, as an LEA nominee and as a co-opted 'expert' respectively.

Current developments in the representation of parents and the evaluation of
their effectiveness need to be seen against the background of a number of contemporary educational and political influences. In the 1980s, a succession of
government Acts has increased the number and status of parents on the governing bodies of schools. Clearly the government thinks it a 'good thing' that
schools should be accountable to parents in this particular way. In this, and other
ways, the present government's view of 'parents' is based on the idea that parents in general are similar to the parents of school-aged children who are also
its own party activists. This is patently *not* the case! As a response to a number
of events and circumstances, such as the teachers' dispute with the government,
declining budgets and their observable effect upon schools and the proposals
contained in the 1987/88 Education Reform Bill, organizations broadly representing the interests of parents have recently been in confrontation with the government, more often than working in partnership with it. There is a slowly
growing recognition, against a wider background, both that current forms of parent representation are rather limited – even stunted – and that, by contrast, there
is much of value to be learned from other countries with different forms and
traditions in this area, such as Italy and Denmark.

Therefore, any general consideration of the representation of the needs and
experience of parents as a whole, would need to look at issues and developments
at the national level, at the local level, and at the school level (see pp.10–11). In
line with the major emphasis of this account as a whole, however, most of the
attention in this section is given to a brief critical review of existing arrangements and possible areas of development at the level of the individual school.
Here, the focus of collective endeavour, of influence and participation, would
not be the governing body, but the parent–school association (the PTA Home–
School Association or Friends of the School), the variety of titles reflects a range
of purposes and aspirations.

School-focused representative bodies, whether joint or otherwise, often seem
to have become the victims of arrested development. For relatively few of these
bodies have grown beyond the fundraising, 'support the school' activities,
whose limited vision has been the subject of sustained criticism. A standard PTA
constitution, whose main purpose is to achieve charitable status so as to avoid
the payment of value added tax on its revenue-producing activities, seems to
symbolize this.

Where there has been growth, it has tended to take the form of a sub-commit-
tee structure with a range of specialist functions, of informal, task-centred
groups and activities within the main body and a tendency to scale down to year
or class groups. Overall, the emphasis is moving towards a programme characterized by range, variety and choice, rather than the three-line-whip for the special event or big occasion.

In the interests of fairness, however, it has to be said that parents and teachers
alike report very different strategies and consequent experience of such bodies.
At worst, they can be cliquish and exclusive; over-concerned with things that
don't matter, and unwilling to take-up those that do; and a collective dummy,
manipulated by the school, for its own purposes. At best, they can be one ele-

ment in a wide-ranging programme, whose main function is to represent the collective interests of parents of children in a particular school; responsive to the needs of parents as a whole, and therefore able to sponsor and support a wide range of activities; and a semi-formal element in a genuine educational partnership, in which parents and teachers each have a voice in the education of the children for whom they are jointly responsible, albeit in different ways.

In looking at the representation of parents as a body, against the wider background of the accountability of schools, the 1986 Education Act provides, probably unwittingly, an important formal link between the representation of parents on school governing bodies and the collective endeavours of parents and teachers generally, through their associations and as part of the home-school programme as a whole. For, as is generally well- known, the Act requires governing bodies to produce an annual report, outlining the school's activities and achievements. This report is then to be presented to a specially called annual meeting of its parents for consideration and discussion. Parents can, if they so choose, vote on proposals that relate to aspects of the report and their implications for future development (including, in the latest Act, the opportunity to opt out of LEA maintained status altogether).

Such proposals seem to me to be dangerously exciting for people with a range of very different philosophies and axes to grind – the realities, however, are so different! For the vast majority of schools, whilst obliged to comply with the letter of the law, do not appear to see it as an opportunity to develop more open home–school relations. Quite the reverse – most schools, deliberately or otherwise, appear to have gone out of their way to limit the flow of information and to play down the possibilities of parental participation and involvement. As a result most annual meetings in the first years of operation have produced abysmally small attendances at meetings that have been characterized by a dreary formality that is a mixture of school governors' meetings and the AGM of the PTA - surely a lethal combination!

At the time of writing it is impossible to say whether such unpromising beginnings, which owe much to their status as legislation imposed by the government without any prior consultation with teachers or parents, will make any positive, longer-term contribution to the development of more effective home–school practice. In terms of the general principles of selection on which this section on current developments has been based, there is a clear need, in considering the representation of parents, to re-examine the basic ground rules, to consider new approaches and, above all, to attempt to develop viable practical alternatives that facilitate joint activity, mutual support and combined effort.

Home–school 'contracts'

Amongst interesting initiatives that are currently emerging in the home–school field, none evokes such strong and widely-differing reactions as the idea of the home–school contract or agreement (a term which lacks the legal force that the former implies). For some, it represents a stick with which to beat parents for their apparent lack of support for the school; for others, it is a stick with which to beat teachers for their apparent unwillingness to take parents seriously. Yet again, it represents a tool in the managerial pursuit of effective forms of appraisal and teacher assessment.

In this context, however, it seems to offer much more constructive potential as a more systematic and, above all, explicit set of agreements about home–school matters, backed up by the appropriate practical arrangements. To even get off the ground it has to be negotiable, clear and realistic. So on the positive side, such an agreement would oblige schools to enter into an active partnership with their parents. But, at the same time, it would make corresponding demands upon parents to exercise their responsibilities amd become actively involved with their children's schools, within agreed areas and limits. It would also focus attention on the relationship between educational intentions and achievements, between fine words and effective action – a recurring theme of this book. But there are also predictable dangers. An obvious criticism is that such an agreement would not be worth the paper it was written on, since in the end, it would be unenforceable. It might also be said to be misleading, or even dishonest, with a tendency to promise things it could not possibly guarantee to deliver. More insidiously, perhaps, it might have the effect – in spite of original intentions to the contrary – of having a narrowing influence, reducing the partnership to the trite and the bland, or to things that are visible or even quantifiable. A practical package, designed to maximize its chances of success, would need to contain the following. (a) Accessible information and evidence, in a variety of appropriate forms concerning: the progress and welfare of individual children; the general activities and achievements of the school, including the problems that need to be tackled. (b) A set of clear practical arrangements: to enable effective, two-way communication to take place between home and school; to initiate, from either side, ways of tackling anxieties and problems, as they arise; to develop forms of mutual support and reciprocal help; and, to encourage parental participation and involvement, in activities that relate both to the development of their own children and to the life and work of the school. (c) An agreed set of purposes, targets and procedures that focus upon children's learning and progress, together with arrangements for their implementation, review and further development. (d) Appropriate mechanisms to pick up and represent the concerns and interests of parents, both individually and collectively.

In the end, however, the success of such initiatives (like much home–school practice) will depend less on their structure and form and more upon the spirit in which they are approached and taken on board and the *context* in which they are developed, particularly in their relationship to the existing experience of parents and teachers in individual schools. For home–school agreements are not likely to work when they are imposed by a general edict or a bland prescription; neither do they represent a sensible starting point for the development of home–school practice. Such initiative is something to work towards, in consolidated stages, thoughtfully along the way. But there can be no denying that such developments represent, potentially at least, a powerful set of opportunities for transforming home–school relations as we know them.

4   Some Issues to Consider

Throughout this book two recurring themes have been given considerable emphasis. In the first place, a view of home–school relations has been developed, which takes into account the perspectives and experience of parents and families, as well as those of teachers and schools. This has fuelled an exploration of ways in which individual schools can respond to such a view and develop the knowledge, attitudes and skills that will enable them to do so, in ways that are both practicable and effective. So, because this is a book for teachers, most of the attention has been given to the planning, organization and evaluation of home–school activities and to the development of both school policy and individual initiative in this area.

This final section, by contrast, offers an opportunity to look at things from a rather different angle, through the examination of a number of issues that have either been overlooked or given relatively little attention, or which come more sharply into focus when viewed from this different, often wider, viewpoint. It also provides a further opportunity to illustrate some of the ways in which professional thinking and practice need to develop together, where the growth of understanding is linked to the capacity to develop effective action. However, in a book of this size, it is not possible to present this in a systematic or comprehensive way. Instead, I have selected a number of issues which echo some of the themes of the series as a whole, from two overlapping areas.

First, family perspectives and experience in general, and developmental perspectives in particular, especially as they relate to the process of schooling. This includes: key moments and special phases in family life; the changing nature of family–school relationships as children get older and pass through the schooling system; important and far-reaching changes that affect family structure, organization and lifestyle. Within this wider view, the more limited concerns of schooling are seen against the broader backcloth of contemporary society with its complex, wide ranging and profoundly changing structures and patterns of behaviour. Here, the health, education and welfare of children and young people is a huge and complex enterprise which, in addition to families themselves, is the concern and responsibility of a wide range of professional and voluntary agencies. In a similar way the relationship between the major institutions of family, school and work continue to be crucially important to the lives of individuals, although these relationships are changing in important ways.

To illustrate some of these themes and issues, I have chosen four linked topics, as follows, to look at briefly, not as abstract issues but in terms of their implications for practice.

(1)   Going from primary to secondary school – to illustrate the idea of key moments and also of continuity and change in family–school relations.

(2)   The role of the pupil in home–school relations – is an example of a very underdeveloped area in the field and also illustrates the gap that can exist between rhetoric and practical action.

(3)   Home–school relations and the organization of family life – which is also a neglected area of considerable practical importance illustrates the changing patterns of family life in ways that bear very directly upon the lives of many children, as most teachers will recognize.

(4)   Inter-agency cooperation – is a constructive response to the relatively untapped possibilities of professionals from different agencies getting together to pool their different kinds of knowledge and experience, in the best interests of children and families.

Key moments: going from primary to secondary school

When we are trying to 'listen to parents' on a large-scale and in a more or less systematic way in our work in Nottingham, we have deliberately tried to bring together two different, but complementary, kinds of experience. The first stems from the continuing, everyday kind of communication and contact between families and schools, often mediated through pupils. Although it is usually indirect, impersonal and implicit, it is nevertheless influential, especially over a period of time.

The concept of 'key moments', by contrast, focuses attention upon particular events and special occasions, often deliberately sought or organized. It is at times like these, such as starting or changing schools, that relationships are made or broken, when important attitudes or patterns of behaviour are laid down for the future. So the idea of 'key moments' can be a useful one in the exploration of home–school thinking and experience across a broad area. It can identify those areas of concern and activity that are common and shared, albeit in different ways, as well as those that are distinctive to either side of the partnership, widely-differing, or even contradictory.

Key moments for teachers, for example, are usually rooted more in the life of the institution, than in the lives of individuals. So a teacher's-eye-view is grounded in events that are part of the organized programmes of schools and of existing attention and effort, however undeveloped. These moments are often organized around the obvious discontinuities of schooling or as a response to important changes, such as changing classes and schools; key events in pupil careers; and the introduction of major changes of personnel, curriculum and organization.

Occasionally, key moments are provided by a crisis in the work or behaviour of particular pupils, classes or teachers, creating the kind of conditions that call for special responses. Key moments for parents and families, by contrast, seem to be more unpredictable and less tied to organized activities. They tend to be rooted more in the lives of members, their personalities and problems of behaviour and development, or the changing circumstances of family life and in the emergence of special moments when 'the penny drops', when parents become able to see things in a clear, formative way, through the catalyst consisting of either a crisis of behaviour involving one of the children; particular encounters with the school and with individual teachers; the arrival of an unexpectedly bad report; sudden realizations, based on comparisons between different children in the same family; or encounters with new subjects, teaching methods or school policies.

The yearly movement of many children from primary to secondary school, provides a useful opportunity to look at a number of these issues and concerns together. For, as well as revealing some of the more important differences between the two major phases of compulsory schooling, it provides an important window into the continuity of family–school relations.

Going from primary to secondary school

> Is there any difference between how easy it is to approach the secondary school, compared to this [primary] school?
>
> Mother In this school you can come in at any time . . . no matter whether you're working or not, you can come in any time and see. If you can't see the teacher you can see Mrs. Thomas [Community teacher], and put your problems to her. But on the senior side you've got to phone up and make an appointment, or take a chance on going down whether the teacher's available or not to see you. If you don't see the teacher, you've got to see the deputy head.

> Are you as familiar with the secondary school?
>
> Mother [Emphatically] No, because it's such a big place and they change teachers every lesson. They aren't staying in one classroom like here . . . so you say go to see a teacher he's had trouble with in Science, or something like that, you go see the teacher, you get lost *looking for* the teacher. Unless you got to, say, the headmaster or deputy head and they appoint a prefect or someone to take you there, you're walking round in circles half the time. I dread going in that side, when it's open night. So it's very awkward – even then when it's open night here you see all the teachers in the classrooms. You got over there you get a list of teachers, you can pick any of the teachers to go and have a word with, but in my son's case, David, he says, 'Go and see Mr. So and So, I like him, I get on alright with him'. So he was giving me a list of teachers he got on with, but he didn't mention the ones that he didn't get on with. So I don't get a true picture of how he is going on, that he doesn't really like . . .
>
> Father . . . We're still involved in what they do. We still like to know what they do, but not quite so involved as we were previously.
>
> Mother Well, we'd got more to do when they were younger because we was teaching them as well. We don't have to now.
>
> Father They're, uh, a bit more independent.

Father   This is possibly one reason why we feel alienated, I think. You could go to Deepdale and whatever you were doing would be discussed, er, it isn't to the same extent at the Comp. but as I say, that could be us . . . don't, don't get the same feeling of welcome down there.

Mother   I don't think the children welcome it. Now up at the infant and the Juniors, you can go up any time and the kids don't bother, but I think, if you went down too often down there, they'd pr'raps call yours 'mardy-baby' you know, and I think that's another reason.

Father   Yeah, the kids aren't over keen on you going too much.

Mother   'Cos I've asked David this. I asked 'Would you sooner I didn't come down, only if I needed to, if anything had gone off?' He said, 'Yes, you don't have to always be coming down to school.'

Father   That's possibly the independence coming out, but erm, it doesn't mean we've got no contact with the school, obviously we have with what David's doing, he keeps us informed of his work, and how he feels about it, but erm, I think I'd like a little bit more contact with the school to enable us to help David at home, so that we p'raps wouldn't feel so out of it when he starts doing something and we get out of our depth.

When primary–secondary transfer takes place, it has a far-reaching effect not only on pupils, but upon their parents and families too. For primary and secondary schools are often very different kinds of places, with their own characteristic forms of organization, respective concerns and ways of doing things. This applies as much to the organization of home–school relations as to other aspects of the life and work of the school.

The anxieties that children and their parents experience when 'going up to the big school', often stem from the size and complexity of secondary schools, particularly for families used to small primary schools; their separation of teaching and caring, in terms of the organization of teachers' responsibilities and efforts; and, the dramatic increase of specialization, making it difficult to keep in touch with children's learning.

For parents, these differences are often amplified by a style of home–school relations that has suddenly become impersonal and bureaucratic, with many sharing responsibility for their children, but no one knowing them well, with most things done through written communication and an appointments system and so on. In these, and other ways, the 'management' of parents has become a more deliberate, obvious and formalized business.

Although many teachers talk as if such problems of transfer are inevitable, our experience has been that schools that recognize such differences and the problems they create, can counter many of them by doing things differently, or at least mitigate some of the worst effects.

For parents, too, the movement from the primary to the secondary phase has both a literal and a symbolic dimension. The literal dimension focuses upon the problems of adjustment to a new larger kind of institution, characterized by the formalism of uniforms and written rules, new kinds of work and ways of working. The parental experience is that individual children will react to, and cope with, these changes in very different ways but that most will, eventually, adjust to the new regime, given enough support and encouragement.

The symbolic dimension of transfer represents a transition in the process of growing up and becoming independent, crossing the bridge from childhood, taking the first steps in learning to cope in the wider, adult world. In such a perspective, transfer symbolises the end of childhood with all that this is likely to mean to parents. If the two dimensions are taken together, 'going up to the big school' merely serves to bring many of the hidden tensions and contradictions that parents experience during their children's schooling crisply into focus.

Some practical suggestions

The planning and organization of a home–school programme will, sooner or later, need to consider the experience of children and their families, as the former pass from primary to secondary schools. For there is much that needs to be done and much that can be done, both in terms of immediate, straightforward action, as well as longer term, more fundamental reform and development of schools themselves.

A good starting point for most secondary schools (but which also applies to many primary schools) is a programme of home–school links that is simpler, more personal and less formal. This might be achieved by using the following methods

- Strengthening the role of the class teacher or form tutor, making him or her the foundation of most communication and contact, on a personal basis. There are many practical ways of reinforcing this, such as the class-based parents' meeting, or a small-scale home-visiting programme. Above all, however it is necessary to make class teachers or form tutors primarily responsible for the day-to-day contact with parents.
- Giving more attention, during transfer, to the more immediate concerns of pupils and their parents, rather than the longer-term consequences of their stay in the school. This might include specially-designed familiarization programmes and procedures, plenty of opportunities for parents to tackle their anxieties at an early stage, in an informal setting. It also requires schools to recognize and use the things that parents know and can do.
- More discussion of the basic routines of the school and particularly of classroom life, of the differences between primary and secondary schools and of the ways in which parents might continue to help their children with their work into the secondary school.
- Broadening professionally-led discussion and activity that focuses upon continuity, liaison and support, to incorporate the natural interest and concern of parents at this stage, in ways that are appropriate to them.

The role of pupils in home–school relations

In the preceding section one of the incidental themes, which is particularly well illustrated in the quotations from parents, concerns the role of pupils in family–school relations and their possible influence. This issue is picked up and developed in the following section, which is followed by the outlining of three

suggestions for the constructive involvement of pupils in home–school practice.

Despite the obvious presence of pupils in the home–school rhetoric, in the
form of teacher:parent:pupil relations, they are almost invariably absent from
its practice. For most home–school activity is carried out, either literally or
metaphorically, behind the backs or over the heads of pupils – almost as if they
didn't exist! There are striking differences between the views of teachers and
parents about the involvement of pupils. Teachers, for example, have very different views about the issue and are deeply divided amongst themselves. For
some, such a practice would be a natural outcome of their present philosophy
and practice, whilst for others it does not seem either relevant or practical. There
are also a good many teachers who fiercely oppose the direct involvement of
pupils, believing strongly that it would compromise, or destroy the point of, for
example, meetings with parents.

Most parents, in direct contrast, find it difficult to formulate a view of home–
school relations in which their children do not have a central and unmistakable
part to play! For much of a parent's view of their children's school and the conditions of classroom life is mediated by their children, both directly and indi-
rectly. In addition, the actual form and content of those relations are formed by
the personality of their children, their basic attitudes to school life and work,
and their success as pupils. So, in these and other ways, pupils are a crucial influence in the very making of home–school relations itself, particularly as they
are experienced by individual families.

The relationship between families and school is, of course, a dynamic, continuously changing one, with young people increasingly active in demanding
their growing independence and becoming increasingly skilled in stage managing the contact between home and school. So pupils can 'lose' notes, set the
agenda for parents' evenings and 'interpret' school reports to their parents. In a
similar way, children can influence the substance and form of their parents' educational knowledge itself as well as their aspirations, attitudes and actions. This
can be a potent form of cultural renewal, not only in the way it imports new
knowledge and skill into the home, but especially in the way school-related
knowledge is used to challenge existing values and patterns of behaviour, either
directly or by setting it against a wider background. This process, characteristically, is strongest when it derives from areas of curriculum and school life which
children either love or hate!

Finally, the spread of pupil involvement in home–school activity provides, in
my view, an exciting example of a professional response to parental views and
experience, rather than the other way round, which is the normal pattern. As
such, it provides an illustration of the possibilities of both two-way communication and genuine partnership.

We have found three main areas of practical activity involving pupils in the
home–school programme, and teachers have adopted them enthusiastically,
with modifications, in the light of experience. There are undoubtedly many
others in what remains a promising, though undeveloped area!

Pupils as interpreters of their work

Mother: If you have a parents' evening, like, you know, I go along then. But I prefer the one where you go along to see the kids' work and they come with you, sort of thing.

Oh yes. What, you take the children?

Mother: Yes, and then they show me their work and they explain it. Instead of going up to the teacher and waiting for him to explain it, I look at the kids' books and then they say what they're doing like.

———————————

Mother: . . . The Michael came home and he explained to me how they actually did . . . work out the answer to the fraction . . . so I think, and knowing that now, you see, I can help Ian when *he* goes on to it.

The process of asking children to explain their work to adults, (usually their parents) is, as has just been mentioned, a strategy drawn from the existing repertoire of many parents. For it is the kind of thing that parents have learned to do for themselves, by improvization, in the home setting. It often develops as a response to particular problems and difficulties, such as the frustrations of maths homework and develops as a technique for subsequent and wider use, perhaps involving other members of the family.

It is a strategy that is of particular use to parents, enabling them to begin to tackle schoolwork-related problems on their own terms, in their own way and, literally, on home ground. It is also likely to yield potential gains to both pupils and their parents. For the former, talking through ideas and experience to an interested adult, in their own language, is a crucial avenue to understanding. For the latter, such a process provides an additional window on classroom life, through the eyes of someone they know well, as well as providing direct evidence of their child as a learner.

As a way of bringing this experience to more parents, legitimizing it and encouraging its fuller use and development, I set up a number of classroom-based sessions with sympathetic schools. We chose areas of concern to parents, such as topic work or maths method and set-up informal, but organized sessions where children would show relevant material to their parents, and explain its use, involve their parents in illustrative activities and discuss any difficulties that arose. This was followed by a cup of tea and an informal discussion with the teacher about the experience, the issues raised and the identification of down-to-earth ways in which parents could continue this kind of work at home.

Such an approach, which is steadily increasing, is generally the work of interested volunteers rather than stemming from a school-wide policy and is useful in providing:
- an opportunity for parents and children to discuss school work together, relating it to actual classrooms
- the possibility of establishing productive links between teacher–parent consultation and the life and work of the classroom generally
- the chance to set-up starting points, targets etc. which parents and children can follow-up, both together and separately

- an emphasis on process and method, rather than the kinds of information that parents are often given, with its emphasis upon marks and grades.

Our experience suggests that when their own children are directly involved, in a friendly and informal setting, parents will attend such sessions in large numbers. However, the issue of parents who are not able to attend, or who do not think it relevant to do so, remains to be tackled, as with other forms of contact.

The direct involvement of pupils in consultation events

Father: I also wonder what it would be like to have the child there as well. It would be interesting to hear what he'd got to say to us – all three of us . . . about how he felt about the school.

When you have a Parents' Evening, is it only parents that are involved, or are the pupils themselves involved?

CC: The pupils sometimes come along to the parents' evenings. They'll wait outside in the House Room and drink coffee with their friends. Um, but when it's me that their parents are talking to, they come in and we talk as a family group . . .

Why do you think that is?

CC: I think some parents have got a good view in many ways. I think when we're talking about an individual's career and what they want to do in the future, which I'm almost always talking about, I think they think it's very important that their child should be involved in any conversation about their future.

Many parents (and some teachers) seem to think that it would be sensible, particularly as children get older, to involve them directly in discussions with teachers and parents about what is, after all, *their* progress! Although it is possible to identify some of the obvious pitfalls and difficulties it does represent an important opportunity to open up the relationship and to ground it firmly in constructive practical action that is tailored to the expressed needs of individuals. The only area where such a practice is currently widespread is in careers sessions in secondary schools and in some FE provision in college courses for school leavers.

The participation of pupils in the preparation of school reports

The direct involvement of pupils in some form of profiling or record keeping is now well-established, largely due to the pressure of DES/MSC initiatives and experience. There are, however, a number of schools that have directly involved pupils in their own self-assessment, in this and other ways, for a number of years.

In one example of such an approach, with which we have been associated (Bosworth College – a Leicestershire 14–18 community college) this is built upon a triangular reporting system, which forms the basis of a continuous dialogue between teachers, parents and students. An examination of such a scheme reveals a number of very significant advantages:

- pupils feel more involved in their own education and more valued as individuals;
- such a process encourages students to feel that they have an important part to play in monitoring their own progress;
- it requires pupils to consider not just what they are learning, but the ways in which they tackle their work;
- such a process can be a valuable means of highlighting problems about which both parents and teachers may have been unaware;
- it provides for the possibility of greater openness, honesty and realism between all three interested parties.

These ideas for practical developments that involve pupils directly in home–school practice in different ways are drawn from a rather patchy and uneven body of experience. They are presented much more in the spirit of illustrating the kind of possibilities that exist, rather than as exemplars of established practice. Like all useful developments that owe something to other people's ideas and experience initially, they need to be thought through and adapted to the needs and circumstances of particular schools, then tried out and modified in the light of that early experience.

Home–school relations and the organization of family life

It often comes as a shock for teachers to realize that the 'cereal packet norm' family, whose children grow up in a more or less settled neighbourhood (within which most of us grew up ourselves) is now in a minority. This section attempts to explore some of the relevant aspects of family life in changing neighbourhoods, in terms of their implications for the development of home–school practice. Such aspects, many of which have yet to be worked through, include:

- the variety of parenting arrangements and styles, which are altering the patterns of bread-winning and caring, conjugal and family relationships and, of course, attitudes towards child-rearing;
- the special needs and problems that stem from family breakdown, separation and divorce, problems of communication and contact that relate to custody and access, the issues raised by re-marriage in 'reconstituted' families etc.;
- the problems and, occasionally, opportunities, created by the effects of long-term unemployment upon family life. A number of these issues, as they might concern schools, for example, were raised in a heightened way during the miners' strike, others are raised by the slow but steady increase in the involvement of fathers in their children's early education;
- the different needs and experience represented by the complexities of family life in multicultural neighbourhoods, particularly where these are reinforced by sharp differences of class, race and culture, by migration and changing patterns of settlement.

From this wide range of complex issues and patterns of change, this section has chosen to explore, as one illustration, some of the practical implications for

schools of marital breakdown and divorce. The justification for this is that, at
any given time, nearly a quarter of all children of school age (regardless of social and geographical background) are involved in such processes. Given the
nature of the issues involved, there also seems to be something of a conspiracy
of silence on the part of the education service about something that affects, often
acutely and for long periods, the lives of so many children in our schools.

As in many areas of family–school relations, this issue is characterized by
widely-differing, contradictory attitudes. Some teachers regard themselves as
'teachers, not bloody social workers', others, perhaps more representative of
teachers generally, accept the need for schools to develop a supportive role, but
feel inadequate because of their lack of training and of appropriate skills.

Similarly, some parents feel it is important that schools are kept in the picture
if their children are to receive the help and support they need; others believe that
divorce is essentially a private matter or that a school's involvement would be
prejudicial to a child's progress in school. Finally, pupils themselves also differ enormously in the extent to which they wish family problems to be generally known about and discussed.

How can schools help?

Schools can help by recognizing the nature and some of the consequences for
children of marital conflict and breakdown and the need to develop: a feel for,
and a tolerance of, the conditions of contemporary family life, in all its forms;
a sensitivity towards the wide-ranging needs of individuals and families; practical arrangements to tackle the issues and special difficulties that are raised;
and, acceptance of the idea that school might be a place where, for example,
separated parents might cooperate in the best interests of their children's education and development.

Paradoxically, schools can also help by learning to recognize – by consultation and experience – the limitations upon schools and teachers in this area:
by being concerned and providing support *without* taking on the responsibility
for solving family problems; by *not* intervening or taking sides in marital disputes; by recognizing that acute or prolonged problems with children require
the resources and experience of other agencies, such as conciliation and counselling services, family welfare groups etc.

Some practical suggestions

1.   Let the curriculum (formal and hidden) reflect the realities of contemporary family life, through social and personal education, RE, history and literature
and so on, but especially through the ways in which parents and families are
referred to in assemblies and in everyday life in classrooms.
2.   Have the issue put on the agenda for a staff meeting or one-off study group
to pool ideas and experience. Consider the possibility of agreeing a set of guidelines and practical ideas. Incorporate parental views and experience.
3.   Identify and encourage the spread of support for children during marital
conflict and breakdown and during re-marriage: examples include making
school a reassuring refuge of normality, making special arrangements to help
with schoolwork-related problems, homework etc. Above all, this can be

achieved by being a sympathetic listener. An important issue here is recognition of the longer-term needs that continue to exist when the family crisis appears to have receded.

4. Review the nature and use of pupil records in relation to problems of keeping them accurate and up-to-date, in responding to information about custody, care and control, access and re-marriage and in relation to matters such as confidentiality.

5. Use pupils to personalize home–school communications so that it is more accurately targeted, as well as making such information more liable to be discussed openly and accepted as normal. Extend information to non-custodial parents concerning:

- reports on children's progress
- invitations to school activities
- access to teachers (jointly or separately, by negotiation) – this would bring schools in the direction of the courts, which increasingly recognize the rights of non-custodial parents to information and access.

A role for LEAs

Given the nature of the problems involved, their implications for schools and other agencies with a shared responsibility for the welfare and development of children, there is probably an important role for local education authorities in:

- recognizing the difficulties that schools experience and offering their support;
- identifying guidelines and practical suggestions for headteachers and their colleagues and for appropriate professionals in other agencies;
- offering practical help in the form of a professional advice centre (perhaps linked to a conciliation and counselling service), INSET opportunities and the general promotion of awareness and thoughtful practice.

Schools and other agencies

This book has consistently been concerned with the relationships between families and schools, particularly those between parents and teachers. It might, then, seem a little strange, even wilful, to close the account by changing the focus to look at a school's relationship with other agencies. However, there are a number of good reasons for doing so.

Such a focus serves as an important and healthy reminder that there is a wide range of agencies in our society who are charged with some kind of responsibility for the health, education and welfare of children and young people. This complex network of roles and services is concerned to: provide and sustain the conditions for healthy growth and orderly development; identify and meet special needs; support employment-related processes; and, provide stimulus and challenge, together with the encouragement, support and resources to take them up.

Against this wider view such agencies, through their different kinds of knowledge, attitudes and skills, throw a light on the processes of contemporary schooling that is often sharply critical of its central preoccupations, values and practices. This can, if acknowledged and used constructively, provide a healthy corrective to that narrowness of vision and concern that is an occupational hazard of schools and those who work in them, that at its worst implies that there are no other worthwhile forms of human existence! Although it is not easily achieved, there is, through the development of cooperation between schools and these other agencies and services, much to be gained, in practical terms, and much to be learned of value, in the development of real education.

Inter-agency cooperation: some suggestions

At the moment, much of the practical cooperation between the statutory and voluntary agencies that work with children and their families is, more often than not, initiated by the school as a crisis measure in relation to behavioural problems.

There will always be the need to develop a mechanism – such as the case conference – to tackle acute problems presented by individual families, as a means of making joint decisions and arriving at action plans for each case. What is also needed, however, is a way of breaking through the model of individual pathologies that can totally dominate such meetings, to be able to pick up and utilize some of the more general lessons, as well as promising lines of collaborative action and development.

In recent years lunchtime meetings, usually based on a secondary school catchment area, have been held as a way of making and sustaining effective professional relationships. These generally informal get-togethers are often supplemented by a series of short contributions, in which individuals describe their work and answer questions about it. This can help to develop a fuller understanding of a wider picture of the relationships between schools and other agencies. Sometimes, however, such groups knit together in such a way as to suggest a Mafia-like collectivity, or a sense of being 'united against a common enemy'! In practice, such groups are likely to reveal both areas of shared concern and practical cooperation, as well as important differences of perspective and approach, where sensitive negotiation will be required.

As publicly-funded activities, the work of health, education and welfare agencies have a responsibility to make the best possible use of their resources of all kinds and to develop the most effective service that they can. At the very least, inter-agency cooperation attempts to minimize wasted, misplaced or duplicated effort. At best, collaborative activity can achieve things with, and on behalf of, children and their families, that are not possible through the efforts of schools and other agencies working alone, let alone in opposition.

An important contribution could be made to inter-agency cooperation through a proposal for its inclusion in initial training and professional development activities. This is particularly relevant to the training of teachers, which is still often carried out in a narrow, isolated way. Inter-disciplinary discussion and practical experience, for example, can reinforce broader notions of schooling, offer a window on a wider range of family and neighbourhood cultures and lifestyles, together with other, often challenging, perspectives on what is normal, characteristic and healthy, both for given communities and for the wider society.

At a practical level, many agencies have much to offer schools and teachers in the development of more broadly-based approaches to teaching and learning.

Experienced professionals working in social work – the youth and probation services, for example – have valuable experience of working with individuals and small groups, through informal styles and in a range of settings.

Finally, there is much to be learned, by teachers and others, from an involvement in broadly-based community projects, particularly where they grow out of the genuine needs of children and young people, their families and neighbourhoods. These projects might have a general brief within a particular neighbourhood, or be targeted towards particular groups, such as the children of families under stress or unemployed school leavers. One of the most valuable features of the best of these projects is that they reject the deficit model of family and community life, in favour of an approach that sets out to identify, and harness, the positive talent and experience that all communities contain.

Such an involvement carries implications for the management of a school's home–school activities and the way these are staffed. At a more formal level, for example, there is a need to link up with the school's head or deputy, and with those specially involved with home–school liaison work, where this applies.

Informally, there are important contributions to be made by members of staff who do youth work, or other kinds of paid work on the premises and in the neighbourhood, at nights and weekends. Finally, there is a special contribution to be made by those who live in the neighbourhood, as well as work in it, because of their access to local knowledge and expertise. All of this, however, is easier said than done! Such important work is particularly difficult to achieve by schools without a special effort, which includes the identification of needs, the allocation of shared tasks and responsibilities and the development of effective resources and continuing support.

The development of more effective home–school practice is, as has been shown throughout this book, an important task for all schools in contemporary society, not an optional extra, as it might previously be said to have been. Whilst this is primarily a task to be tackled by individual schools, through the improvement of their work with the families of the children they teach, it is too big a job for schools alone. It requires the involvement and support, both of the education service as a whole and of the range of agencies that share some of the professional responsibility for the health, education and welfare of children and young people. Above all, however, such a task is impossible without the active cooperation, support and involvement of parents and families themselves, a task which has provided a mainspring, not only of this book but of the series as a whole.

5 Some Useful Resources

'Parents and Teachers' series – John Bastiani, NFER-NELSON

Working with Parents: A whole-school approach is the third book in a series which attempts to bring together a wide range of material, much of it specially written, on the theme of relations between parents and teachers. Its main over-all purpose is to contribute to both a better understanding of complex home–school issues and, as a consequence, to the development of more effective thinking and practice. The different volumes, although very different in form and content, are linked by a shared underlying philosophy which attaches im-portance to the perspectives and experience of parents – hence the series title.

In the first volume, *Perspectives On Home–School Relations*, considerable emphasis is given to the problems of studying home–school relations, and of thinking through a number of related issues and concerns of current professional interest. In these accounts, an attempt has been made to provide a broad view of the field, through challenging material which explores its essentially proble-matic nature and illustrates some of the more salient features of issue, perspec-tive and method.

The second volume, *From Policy to Practice*, carries on where the previous volume leaves off. Here emphasis has been given to both the major concerns of both policy makers and practitioners and, particularly, to the processes through which we attempt to translate ideas into effective action – a task which is de-veloped, in a very different style, in the present book.

'The Development of Effective Home–School Programmes' project

This enterprise – which is not a project in the conventional sense – began in 1976 and is still in existence, based in the School of Education at the Univer-sity of Nottingham. It consists of a developing programme of research and de-velopment work, of teaching and study and, above all, of in-service work with parents and teachers. Whilst it has generated a considerable number and variety of publications, readers of the present book are more likely to be interested in the following:

ATKIN, J. and BASTIANI, J. (with GOODE, J.). *Listening To Parents: an approach to the improvement of home/school relations.* Beckenham: Croom-Helm.

In many ways, this is the best guide to the essential concerns and activities of the Nottingham home–school approach.

ATKIN, J. and BASTIANI, J. (1984). *Preparing Teachers to Work with Parents: a survey of initial training.* Nottingham: Nottingham University School of Education.

An analysis of the actual and potential role of training and professional development in the home–school field.

ATKIN, J. and BASTIANI, J. (1984). *Home and School: A Studyguide.* Nottingham: Nottingham University School of Education.

A brief, very compressed introduction to the home–school literature and its wide-ranging concerns.

BASTIANI, J. (Ed) (1978). *Written Communication Between Home and School. A report by the Community Education Working Party.* Nottingham: Nottingham University.

COMMUNITY EDUCATION WORKING PARTY (1983) *Teacher/Parent Interviews: some materials for teachers.* Nottingham: Nottingham University.

Two complementary reports, looking at written and face-to-face communication respectively, produced by a working group of teachers based on the School of Education at the University of Nottingham.

BASTIANI, J. (1986). *Your Home/School Links.* Keyworth, Notts.: New Education Press.

A short, readable booklet containing a large number of practical ideas and suggestions.

Some further suggestions for reading

The home–school literature is extensive, varied and growing steadily. Here are some of the more accessible accounts, representing each of the major phases, which also have considerable practical application.

BECHER T. *et al.* (1981). *Policies for Educational Accountability.* London: Heinemann.

ELLIOTT, J. *et al.* (1981). *Schools Accountability.* London: Grant-McIntyre.

JOHNSON, D. and RANSOM, E. (1983). *Family and School.* London: Croom Helm.

MACBETH, A. (1984). *The Child Between: A Report on School–Family Relations in the Countries of the European Community.* Luxemburg Office for Official Publications of the European Communities: HMSO.

McCONKEY, R. (1985). *Working With Parents: A Practical Guide for Teachers and Therapists.* London: Croom Helm.

NATIONAL CONSUMER COUNCIL (1986). *The Missing Links Between Home and School: A Consumer View.* London: NCC.

TIZARD, B. *et al.* (1981). *Involving Parents in Nursery and Infant Schools.* London: Grant McIntyre.

WOLFENDALE, S. (1983). *Parental Participation in Children's Development and Education.* London : Gordon and Breach.

Useful organizations and their publications

The Advisory Centre for Education (ACE), 18 Victoria Park Square, Bethnal Green, London E2 9PB. ACE is a long-established voice for the concerns of parents of school-aged children. It publishes a very useful regular bulletin (formerly 'Where') which provides useful information and ideas. It also orchestrates and endorses campaigns, such as open access to pupil records or opposition to corporal punishment in schools.

The National Confederation of Parent/Teacher Associations (NCPTA), 43 Stonebridge Road, Northfleet, Gravesend, Kent DA11 9JW. The NCPTA publishes a regular newsletter, 'The Parent Teacher', and has recently become bolder in commissioning and publishing inquiries into matters of parental concern, such as 'The State of Our Schools'. It consists of a federation of county and local groups, which vary a great deal in character and liveliness. It is connected with a publishing wing, the *Home and School Council* which produces very readable, down to earth booklets on a wide-range of home–school topics.

The Pre-school Playgroups Association (PPA), Alford House, Aveline Street, London SE11 5DH. The PPA produces material for playgroups and parents of pre-school children. It has a well- developed training and advisory network and does excellent work in involving ordinary parents in a voluntary capacity.

There are also a number of important *national resource centres* which, although having distinctive concerns and responsibilities, share a number of common features, such as:

- a broad concern for the development of both policy and practice in their respective areas;
- act as an agent in the commissioning of research and development work in important or neglected areas;
- coordinate information and disseminate experience from the field;
- encourage the growth of inter-professional collaboration and activity, at all levels.

The Community Education Development Centre, based at Briton Road, Coventry, CV2 4LF. The Community Education Development Centre has a varied and extensive involvement in the development of more effective home–school policy and practice. Of particular interest here are its publications and especially its monthly newsletter, 'Network', which is an invaluable guide to the current scene, very readable and a continuing reminder of both the force of home–school ideals and the range and diversity of current practice.

The National Children's Bureau at 8 Wakley Street, London EC1V 7QE. The National Children's Bureau gives emphasis to the development of parenting and family life. It concentrates its energies on the needs of younger children and their families, particularly those that are confronted by the disadvantage and difficulties engendered by contemporary urban life.

The National Youth Bureau, Albion Street, Leicester. The National Youth Bureau, while less obviously concerned with home–school matters, focuses upon needs and concerns of young people in our society, especially, from the vantage point of this book, with the educational, family and working lives of school leavers.

Other organisations include:

Campaign for the Advancement of State Education (CASE), Press Officer, 25 Leybourne Park, Kew Gardens, Richmond, Surrey. CASE works through local groups campaigning for improvements in state education.

Education Otherwise, Field House, Mellis Road, Thrandeston, Diss, Norfolk. Education Otherwise offers advice and contacts to parents wishing to educate their children in family and other non-school settings.

National Association of Governors and Managers (NAGM), 81 Rustlings Road, Sheffield S11. The NAGM is currently very active in the training of school governors and managers, and as a pressure group for their interests.

The National Consumer Council (NCC), 18 Queen Anne's Gate, London, SW1H 9AA. The NCC has become interested in education only fairly recently. It is making up for lost time, however, with interest developing in its Scottish, Welsh and English bodies.

Additional sources of ideas and experience

Educational Libraries (Universities, Polytechnics and HE Institutes) contain appropriate books, journals and magazines. Increasingly, home–school topics are the focus of course work at all levels and more of this seems to be applied and of practical relevance, rather than narrowly academic. Public libraries are more unpredictable but have very effective request systems.

Teachers Centres have, or can usually be persuaded to set-up loan collections of relevant project reports, teacher INSET materials etc. They can also be responsive to suggestions from teachers for professional development activities in the home–school area, which are shaped by the expressed needs and concerns of teachers themselves.

The Educational Press tends to reflect a wide range of different values in its handling of home–school matters, but often does little more than reflect stereotyped views and prejudices uncritically. More thoughtful treatment can be found, however, in the *Times Educational Supplement* and the *Education Guardian* (published on Tuesdays).

Also from NFER-NELSON

Parents and Teachers 1: Perspectives on Home-School Relations
Edited by John Bastiani

Interest in the relationship between family and school has increased dramatically in recent years, with growing pressure from government and parents for more parental involvement in schools. However, there is little or no guidance for teachers about the nature and extent of their duties in this area.

Parents and Teachers 1: Perspectives on Home-School Relations is the first of three linked volumes which explore this problematic relationship. This volume is a collection of readings, drawn from a range of academic orientations and disciplines, which addresses the key issues under debate. It examines the place of home-school relations in the wider social system and goes on to look in detail at the parent-teacher relationship. In the final part of the book, issues of current concern, such as management, special needs and multicultural education, are discussed with reference to the home-school relationship.

Parental involvement is one of the most controversial areas of debate in education today. A valuable primer for anyone wanting to make themselves familiar with a range of different approaches to the subject.

ISBN 0 7005 1131 8

For further information, please contact our
Customer Support Department on (0753) 858961,
or write to the following address:

NFER-NELSON, Darville House,
2 Oxford Road East, Windsor,
Berkshire SL4 1DF

Also from NFER-NELSON

**'Race' and the Primary School
Theory into Practice**
Bruce Carrington and Geoffrey Short

Draws on case study material to address the practical
difficulties which teachers face when implementing
antiracist, multicultural initiatives, examining in
particular the needs of 'all-white' schools. The book
concludes with an examination of the implications for
initial and in-service teacher education.

Hardback 0 7005 1196 2   Paperback 0 7005 1197 0

Managing Mathematics in the Primary School
Marion Stow

Provides the Mathematics Coordinator with a practical
resource for improving the teaching of mathematics in
schools. From the role of the coordinator to training
and support, each area covered is followed by
activities and exercises which may be photocopied if
necessary. An ideal companion to the NFER
Research Library title, *Mathematics Coordination: A
study of practice in primary and middle schools.*

0 7005 1210 1

Self-evaluation: A Primary Teacher's Guide
Janet R. Moyles

Approaches the subject of accountability from the
primary teacher's point of view and argues for the
benefits of effective self-evaluation. The author has
developed a self-evaluation model in the form of a
checklist which enables teachers to assess their
performance in the classroom and to evaluate their
wider role within the school. A photocopy master of
this model is provided in the back of the book.

0 7005 1180 6

For further details concerning the above
titles, please contact our Customer Support
Department on Windsor (0753) 858961.

 NFER-NELSON, Darville House,
2 Oxford Road East, Windsor,
Berkshire SL4 1DF

Books from NFER-NELSON

**Learning Difficulties in Reading and Writing:
A Teacher's Manual**
Rea Reason and Rene Boote

'Full of practical approaches for teachers and parents
working with children experiencing basic learning
difficulties... I would strongly recommend this as a
'survival kit' for any teacher of a child with basic
literary difficulties.'

Special Children

'Includes an excellent chapter on spelling and
sensitive treatment of handwriting.'

Times Educational Supplement

0 7005 1072 9

**Special Needs in the Primary School:
Identification and Intervention**
Lea Pearson and Geoff Lindsay

'A clear, concise, readable account of what primary
teachers need to know concerning the implications for
them of the 1981 Act.'

Educational Psychology

The authors provide an overall problem solving
framework for special needs support and discuss
specific approaches to identification.

0 7005 1005 2

Expertise and the Primary School Teacher
Philip H. Taylor

Explores the nature of curriculum responsibility in the
primary school in relation to the role of the teacher
and the changing character of primary education this
century. The book addresses the central question: how
much a curriculum generalist and how much a subject
specialist should the primary school teacher be?

0 7005 1036 2

For further details concerning the above
titles, please contact our Customer Support
Department on Windsor (0753) 858961.

NFER-NELSON, Darville House,
2 Oxford Road East, Windsor,
Berkshire SL4 1DF